HOME WIRING

Albert Jackson and David Day

Hearst Books
A Division of Sterling Publishing Co., Inc.
New York

Popular Mechanics

Steve Willson, U.S. Project Editor
Tom Klenck, U.S. Art Director

Created, edited, and designed by Inklink

Concept, editorial, design and art direction: Simon Jennings
Text: Albert Jackson and David Day
Design: Alan Marshall
Illustrations: David Day, Robin Harris, Brian Craker, Michael Parr, Brian Sayers
Photographs: Paul Chave, Peter Higgins, Simon Jennings, Albert Jackson

Hearst Books

Project editor: Joseph Gonzalez
Cover design: Celia Fuller

Library of Congress Cataloging-in-Publication Data available.

10 9 8 7 6 5 4 3 2 1

Published by Hearst Books
A Division of Sterling Publishing Co., Inc.
387 Park Avenue South, New York, NY 10016

Popular Mechanics and Hearst Books are registered trademarks of Hearst Communications, Inc.

www.popularmechanics.com

For information about custom editions, special sales, premium and corporate purchases, please contact Sterling Special Sales Department at 800-805-5489 or specialsales@sterlingpub.com.

Distributed in Canada by Sterling Publishing
c/o Canadian Manda Group, 165 Dufferin Street
Toronto, Ontario, Canada M6K 3H6

Sterling ISBN-13: 978-1-58816-533-6
        ISBN-10: 1-58816-533-7

Contents

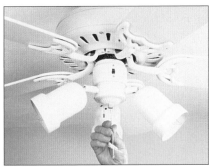

Electricity in our homes

Electricity has been so much a part of our lives for so many years that now it's hard to imagine living without it. We instinctively reach for a switch in the dark and a light comes on. We give little thought to circuitry, to switches, to the flow of current. We expect it to be there, and most of the time it is. Only when our electrical systems fail do we give them much thought. And then we are likely to be more confused than curious. For many of us, it all seems an unapproachable mystery. Electricity sounds dangerous, and any discussion of it seems hopelessly and deliberately obscured by difficult technical jargon.

The truth of the matter is that electricity is complicated when used to do complicated things, as in advanced electronics. But you don't have to start at that level. You can start with the simplest repair and work up.

Electricity is learnable because it is logical and sequential, and therefore predictable. Electrical current runs along wires as simply as water passes through plumbing pipes. Switches interrupt current just as valves and faucets interrupt water. If this analogy seems too simple, it probably is, but learning to think in simple progressions is the key to understanding your home's electrical system.

Like so many other areas of home improvement, electrical projects are now made easier with improved materials. Manufacturers are designing more and more items with the inexperienced do-it-yourselfer in mind. In many ways, electrical work has never been easier. Start by doing the little things. Small projects will give you the confidence to approach larger projects. Eventually, doing your own electrical work will offer real savings and the satisfaction of greater self-sufficiency.

Think safe to be safe

Don't overload circuits

Use screw for adapter

Test for current

One of the most intimidating aspects of electricity is its ability to injure or even kill. With a few precautions, however, you can eliminate the danger factor and work without fear of being hurt. In fact, you are probably more likely to electrocute yourself through careless living habits than when attempting a do-it-yourself wiring project. The following list of dos and don'ts will protect you from electrical hazards, both in your daily living and when working on your home's electrical system.

- Always shut the power off at the main service panel to any circuit you intend to work on.
- Do not overload a receptacle with adapters and extension cords.
- Do not run extension cords under carpets or throw rugs. Constant traffic can fray a cord's insulation, creating a fire hazard.
- When holding electric razors, hair dryers, or any bath or kitchen appliance, do not touch faucets or plumbing pipes, as most electrical systems are grounded through the plumbing system.
- When bathing, keep radios, hair dryers, and other small appliances a safe distance from the tub.
- When adapting a three-prong plug to a two-prong receptacle, make sure the adapter is grounded to the screw on the receptacle's coverplate and that the box is grounded.
- When a fuse blows, never install a substitute fuse with an amperage rating greater than the one you are replacing.
- Do not pull a plug from a receptacle by its cord. The cord will soon tear loose inside the plug, overheat, and become a fire hazard.
- Always unplug an appliance or lamp before attempting a repair.
- Before starting any work, use a voltage tester to make sure the power is off. A lamp or small appliance will also work in testing outlets for power.
- Do not use aluminum ladders when working near overhead service lines or when testing live circuits.
- If you must work on wet floors, wear rubber boots and stand on planks to provide a buffer between you and the moisture.
- Because most electrical systems are grounded through metal plumbing systems, never touch plumbing pipes while working on electrical projects.
- When making plumbing repairs, make sure that you do not splice a length of plastic pipe into a plumbing line that also serves as a grounding conductor.

Even if you understand nothing about the wiring in your home, you can still save on energy consumption by following these basic conservation measures.

Kitchen

- Use flat-bottom pans roughly the same size as the burner when cooking on electric range tops.
- Cover foods when boiling to speed the heating process and reduce energy consumption.
- Use microwaves when possible, as they cook faster and use less wattage.
- When hand-washing dishes, use a sink stopper to hold water. A continually running hot rinse uses much more water.
- Clean dust and grease from refrigerator condensers at least three times a year. Dirty condensers are very inefficient to operate.

Heating and cooling

- Set thermostats at 68° F in winter and 78° F in summer. Each degree under 68° F and over 78° F will save approximately 3 percent of your total heating or cooling costs.
- Open drapes facing the sun during the day in winter and close them during the day in summer. In wintertime, close all drapes at night to reduce heat loss.
- Apply caulk and weather stripping to leaky windows and doors to further reduce heat loss.

Laundry and bath

- Wash only full loads of clothing. When possible, wash with warm water and rinse with cold water.
- Because clogged filters interrupt efficient airflow, clean dryer lint filters after every load.
- Showers generally require less hot water than baths. To reduce further the amount of hot water needed, install a simple volume-reduction washer in the showerhead.
- Repair leaky faucets, as they can cost you hundreds of gallons of hot and cold water each year.

Waterbeds

- The heater in an unmade waterbed can consume 30 percent more energy than when the bed is fully covered.

Until you understand the basics of electricity, your electrical skills will be limited to simple repair projects. Luckily, once you get past the usual apprehensions, electricity is quite easily understood. Electricity is logical and so can be learned in small steps. The basics are explained on this page.

Volts × Amps = Watts

The electrons flowing through a circuit cause a current measured in amperes. The rate of flow can vary greatly, according to demand and power source. Current flows only when called for by an appliance. Amperes are moved along the circuit by pressure, called voltage. When we multiply voltage (pressure) times amperes (current) we get wattage, which is a measure of how much electricity is being used. If the current passes through a 75-watt bulb, for example, the electricity consumed, or pulled out of the current, will be 75 watts. Similarly, a 1500-watt electric space heater consumes 1500 watts of power.

Amperes

Amperes, often shortened to amps, are precise units of measurement. Approximately 6¼ billion billion electrons moving past a point in a circuit each second equals 1 amp. Among many other things, amps are used to rate appliances, power tools, and your home's electrical circuits. A typical service panel will carry a variety of circuits with different amp ratings, usually between 15 and 50 amps.

Volts

Just as water pressure is measured in pounds, electrical pressure is measured in volts. The greater the voltage, the greater the pressure behind the amperes. Some voltage is lost when forced through a long conductor. This reduction is called resistance. Although a short and a long conductor might have the same voltage input, the long conductor will deliver a lower output. The difference in output is the amount of current lost to the inherent resistance of the wire.

When voltage arrives at your service panel, it may fluctuate. This voltage ebb and flow may vary as much as ten or twelve units. You could be receiving from 114 to 126 volts at any given time. To establish some workable standard, the writers of the National Electrical Code established two systems: 120 and 240 volts. Today, all electrical materials are designed to these standards and rated accordingly.

Watts

Watts measure how much power is being used at a given time. To size a circuit and breaker, you must first determine the maximum wattage needed for a given room or group of rooms. We do this by adding up the watts as listed on light bulbs and appliances. A normal kitchen circuit might be quickly overloaded by a refrigerator, microwave, and a few small appliances.

We also need to know how many watts a 15- or 20-amp breaker will deliver, so we multiply 15 amps times 120 volts, to get 1800 watts of potential power. If your maximum anticipated wattage is more than 1800, extra circuits will be necessary.

Watt-hours are also the measure used by power companies to keep track of the electricity we use. To make the billing more manageable, watt-hours are calculated in units of one thousand, known as kilowatt-hours. Each Kwh equals 1000 watt-hours, as measured by your service meter.

A simple circuit

For electricity to work, you must establish a circuit. A circuit is simply a wire loop that travels from an electrical source to an electrical outlet and back. Billions of electrons flow down one side of the loop, through the outlet and back along the other side. Only when a loop remains closed can electricity flow through it. If the loop is interrupted, as with a switch, the flow stops. The electrons must travel full circle to create a current. When a circuit is incomplete, it is said that a "short" exists. This can be the result of a broken wire or an improper connection.

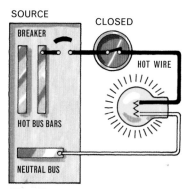

Closed loop
When switch is closed, current flows

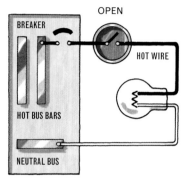

Open loop
When switch is open, current cannot flow

240-volt circuits
Many major appliances such as clothes dryers, water heaters, and air conditioners require more voltage than can be handled by 120-volt conductors. To accommodate these greater voltage needs, two 120-volt circuits are joined in the service panel to create a single 240-volt circuit. Of course, 240-volt conductors, or cables, are often heavier to withstand the extra amperage.

Low-voltage circuits

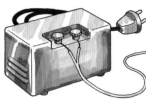

Transformer

Low-voltage wiring has long been used for doorbells and thermostats because they require so little energy. Recently, however, low-voltage systems have become popular in indoor track lighting and in landscape lighting as well. Low-voltage systems operate on approximately 12 volts. To reduce from 120 volts to 12 or fewer volts, small transformers are used. These transformers are usually supplied with low-voltage kits.

Codes and the grandfather clause

What if you are adding wiring to a home that does not meet current code requirements? When the inspector sees the existing wiring, will he make you upgrade it as well? The answer is almost always no. As codes change, you are not expected to change your home's wiring too. If your home was wired to code when it was built or remodeled, it falls under the grandfather clause. Only those sections you alter (and those sections affected by the alteration) must meet current code specifications.

Of course, there are exceptions. If existing wiring poses a serious threat to property and lives, you can be required to correct the problem.

About the NEC

The first electrical code in this country was proposed in 1881 by the National Association of Fire Engineers. It was written in response to the many fires started by electricity then. It had only three rules. As we came to understand more about electricity, the code was expanded. The NEC guidebook is now a dense and highly technical book. Over 1000 revisions were made in each of the last few updates. Today it is considered a legal document, which makes it almost unreadable by amateurs. For the pertinent information it contains, buy instead, one of the simplified guidebooks available at bookstores.

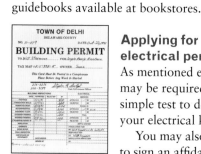

Applying for an electrical permit

As mentioned earlier, you may be required to take a simple test to demonstrate your electrical know-how.

You may also be required to sign an affidavit stating that you are the owner of the home listed in the permit application. If the home is not yours, don't expect to receive a permit. The house must be yours, and it must be a single-family dwelling. If it is a multifamily, you will not be issued a permit.

When a permit is issued to you, you must display it where it can be seen from the street. In most cases, you will have a year to complete the work, but expect inspectors to start looking in after a month or two.

How much should you do?

If you own a single-family home, you can legally work on any of the electricity on your side of the meter. This does not mean that you can invent your own standards, however. The next person to live in your house has a right to be protected against dangerous or substandard workmanship and materials. It does mean that if you work to accepted standards, as defined by the National Electrical Code, you cannot be prohibited from doing your own wiring. All that is required is a work permit and a series of on-site inspections by code officials. Every major wiring project should begin with a visit to your local codes office for a consultation with officials.

When do you need a permit?

You need a permit any time you alter or add to existing wiring. You will also need a permit when wiring major home appliances or when installing any outdoor or outbuilding wiring. When wiring will be covered up by finished walls or ceilings, a "rough-in" inspection is required, in addition to a "finish" inspection upon completion. Simple repairs, such as replacing switches and receptacles, generally do not require permits. When in doubt, call your municipal or county codes office.

Your local code authority will be happy to supply the forms you will need to apply for a permit. Inspectors are not hard to work with until you cross them. You will be charged a small fee to defray the costs of inspection, and in some cases you may be required to take a simple test to demonstrate your understanding of basic electrical principles. The test is not difficult. This chapter will give you more than enough information to pass it. Many authorities do not even require a test.

You may also be required to supply a rough drawing of the work you have in mind. Don't panic; this drawing need not be complicated, and besides, it offers the perfect opportunity for you to clarify any technical questions you might have.

UL listings

Just as you should maintain the highest standards of work-manship, you should use safe and tested materials. The best way to find quality materials is to look for a UL listing or the approval stamp of another major domestic testing laboratory. Electricity is only as safe as the materials used to bring it to you. A small savings on unapproved materials could cost you plenty in property damage or personal injury.

Property insurance and your wiring

Home insurance policies are not likely to include exclusionary clauses concerning your electrical work. Even so, if a fire starts in your home and can be directly tied to your faulty electrical work, your insurance company may consider you a permanent bad risk and decide not to renew your policy.

Similar complications can result from work performed in your home by a licensed electrician who has not obtained a permit.

Furthermore, you may be liable to a future owner of your home under the latent-defect laws of your state. If you knowingly hide an electrical defect when the contract is signed, the future owner can sue you for damages after the sale, or at least require you to correct the problem.

Conversely, acquiring a permit and setting up the proper inspections is the best insurance policy you can have. Once your code authority approves your work, you are in the clear. Any questions of liability will be directed elsewhere.

In short, acquire permits and follow code regulations. Codes protect you and the person who buys your home when you move on. In most cases, wiring to code does not make your work any more difficult or expensive, just safer. It only makes good sense to wire your home in the safest way.

Basic electrical toolbox

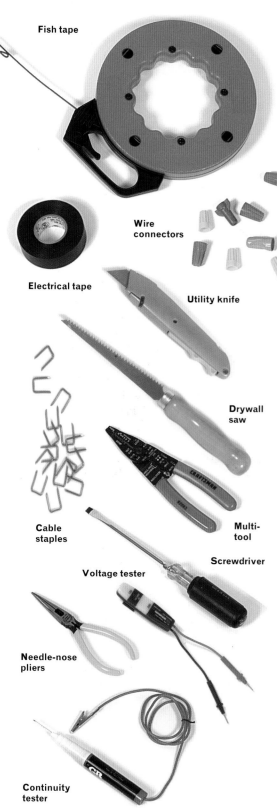

Fish tape

Wire connectors

Electrical tape

Utility knife

Drywall saw

Multi-tool

Screwdriver

Cable staples

Voltage tester

Needle-nose pliers

Continuity tester

Many homeowners are intimidated by the prospect of electrical repairs, though they really shouldn't be. When approached safely, and with the proper tools, basic repairs and installations are quite easy and involve little risk. Bookstores, home centers, and magazines abound with information on basic electrical projects, and with some study, even complicated upgrades are within the reach of most do-it-yourselfers. There isn't much about electrical work that is physically demanding, but the right selection of tools will make any job easier.

The good news is that assembling a basic electrical toolkit isn't very hard because it includes relatively few tools. And the total cost of these tools is often less than the cost of a single service call by an electrician. Your tool kit may vary slightly, depending on your specific needs. But the tools and accessories shown here make a good starting point for most people. When supplemented by other, more common household tools, you'll be able to tackle most jobs successfully. Of course, any major project will require a permit beforehand and an electrical inspection afterward to conform to local codes.

The tools you'll need

Fish tape
This tool has a rigid coil of metal tape wound around a retractable wheel. It's used for pulling new cable within finished floors, walls, and ceilings.

Electrical tape
Plastic tape is flexible, durable, and easy to use. For making minor repairs on damaged cable sheathing, and for holding cable to the end of a fish tape, it can't be beat.

Utility knife
This tool has more uses than can be listed. It's the best tool for cutting and stripping cable sheathing.

Wire connectors
Available in different sizes to match the wires being joined, these small devices twist wires together and hold them securely.

Drywall saw
You don't need this if you already have a keyhole saw. But it's made specifically for cutting holes in drywall.

Multi-tool
This tool is the heart of the toolkit. It can cut cable and wires and can strip wires cleanly without damaging the copper under the insulation.

Cable staples
Staples are required to fasten new cable to studs and joists.

Screwdriver
Only one flat-blade screwdriver is shown here. But you'll need an assortment of sizes in both flat blade and Phillips heads.

Voltage tester
This tool has two wire probes joined by a small neon light. It's used to determine if power is present in a receptacle, switch, or any wire in any circuit. When current passes through the probes, it lights the bulb.

Needle-nose pliers
These pliers are used for any number of small tasks, but are particularly useful for bending the ends of wire to fit around a terminal screw.

Continuity tester
This two-probe tool differs from a voltage tester because it has its own battery power source. It's used primarily to find out if a device is working. When the clip is put on one side of a device (a switch, for instance) and the probe is touched to the other side, a circuit is completed. If the tool lights, it means the device is working.

From the source to you

Upgrading your service

Electricity is created by generators that may be powered by water, oil, gas, coal, or nuclear reactor. From these generators electricity is pumped to distribution stations at very high pressure, or voltage. From the distribution stations, the voltage is reduced, split and distributed to major cities and rural areas.

From a local substation, electricity is pumped down your street, either through overhead or underground cables. Each home is then attached to this main line by means of a residential service conductor. An older home might have a two-wire service capable of carrying only 30 amps of power at 120 volts of pressure. Homes built in the last 30 years are likely to have three-wire services capable of carrying from 60 to 200 amps at 120/240 volts.

With today's increased electrical needs, 30-amp services are seldom adequate. If you are willing to upgrade your service panel and possibly your home wiring, you can have your electrical supplier install an upgraded three-wire service. Some municipalities will allow you to install your own service panel, but installing a new weather head, meter, and service conductor should always be left to a professional. To determine if you will need upgraded wiring to accommodate a new service and panel, contact an electrician, your power company, or your local code authority. In any case, strict adherence to code specifications is a must.

One of the advantages of installing a new service is that you can usually convert from an overhead to an underground cable. Overhead services, called service drops, detract from the appearance of a home and are subject to storm damage. Overhead services can also kill you if you touch them with aluminum ladders or tree-pruning equipment. Even if you have an overhead three-wire service, you can have your power company convert it to an underground service, called a "service lateral," for a fee. Of course, your yard must be large enough to allow a trencher to maneuver. Patios and other large expanses of concrete also get in the way of trenches and may prohibit going underground.

Service lateral
1 Service entrance meter
2 Meter grounding conductors
3 Grounding electrode
4 Water pipe
5 Underground conduit riser

Electrical supply network

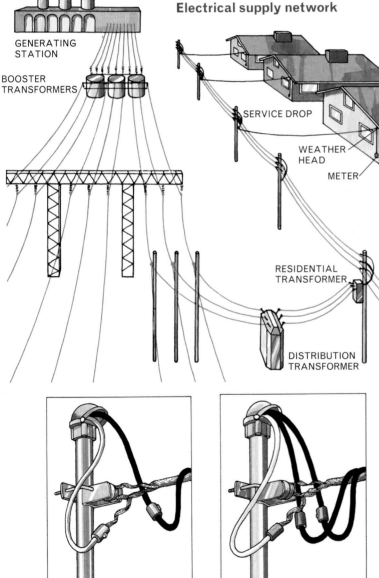

GENERATING STATION

BOOSTER TRANSFORMERS

SERVICE DROP

WEATHER HEAD

METER

RESIDENTIAL TRANSFORMER

DISTRIBUTION TRANSFORMER

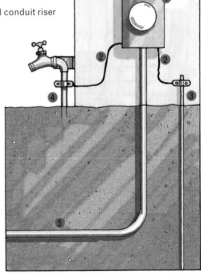

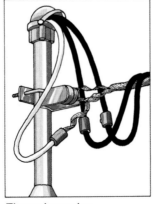

Two-wire service

Three-wire service

How we use the electricity we buy

The rates listed below are for a specific area. Yours will be higher or lower.
Information supplied by the Lincoln Electric System, Lincoln, Nebraska.

CONSUMPTION AND COSTS FOR COMMON

Appliance	Average Wattage	Avg. Hrs. Per Mo.	Avg. Kwh Per Mo.	Avg. Cost Per Mo.	Avg. Cost Per Hour
Food preparation					
Blender	386	3.2	1.24	$ .07	2.3¢
Coffee Maker (drip)					
Brew	1440	3.0	4.32	$ .26	8.7¢
Warm	85	240.0	20.40	$ 1.23	.5¢
Deep Fryer	1448	4.7	6.80	$ .41	8.8¢
Electric Frying Pan	1196	13.0	15.50	$ .94	7.2¢
Electric Knife	92	1.0	.09	$ .01	.6¢
Garbage Disposer	445	6.0	2.70	$ .16	2.7¢
Microwave	1500	11.0	16.50	$ 1.00	9.1¢
Mixer (hand)	127	1.0	.13	¢ .01	.8¢
Toaster	1146	3.0	3.40	$ .21	6.9¢
Toaster Oven	1500	2.0	3.00	$ .18	9.1¢
Broiler	830	6.0	5.00	$ .30	5.0¢
Oven	1500	11.0	16.50	$ 1.00	9.1¢
Range					
bake	2833	8.0	22.70	$ 1.37	17.1¢
Broil	2900	6.0	14.70	$ 1.05	17.5¢
Surface Units					
6"-unit, high setting	1400	—	—	—	8.5¢
8"-unit, high setting	2600	—	—	—	15.7¢
Sandwich Grill	1161	2.3	2.67	$ .16	7.0¢
Slow Cooker	200	57.0	11.40	$ .69	1.2¢
Waffle Iron	1161	1.6	1.90	$ 11	7.0¢
Food preservation					
Freezer					
15 cu. ft. upright	341	262.0	99.60	$ 6.02	2.1¢
15 cu. ft. upright frostless	440	334.0	147.00	$8.89	2.7¢
Refrigerator/Freezer					
15 cu. ft.	326	291.0	94.90	$5.74	2.0¢
15 cu. ft. frostless	615	248.0	152.50	$9.23	3.7¢
Utility					
Central Vacuum System	4300	8.0	34.40	$ 2.08	26.0¢
Clock	2	730.0	1.46	$ .09	—
Dishwasher	1200	25.0	30.00	$ 1.82	7.3¢
Dryer	4856	17.0	83.00	$ 4.99	29.4¢
Fluorescent Light (40w)	40	92.0	3.68	$ .22	.2¢
Fluorescent Light (20w)	20	92.0	1.84	$ .11	.1¢
Incandescent Light (100w)	100	92.0	9.20	$ .56	.6¢
Iron	1100	12.0	13.00	$ .80	6.7¢
Sewing Machine	75	12.0	.90	$ .05	.5¢
Vacuum Cleaner	630	6.0	3.80	$ .23	3.8¢
Washing Machine (automatic)	512	17.0	8.70	$ .53	3.1¢
Water Bed (king size, operating 50% of the time)	375	321.0	120.00	$7.28	2.3¢
Water Heater	4500	111.0	500.00	$ 30.22	27.0¢

Summer rate=7.15¢/Kwh   Winter rate=4.9¢/Kwh   Average=5.7¢/Kwh

Meters and service entrances

All the electricity you use is recorded in Kwh by your meter. You can actually watch older meters count. A numbered disc spins when electricity is used and the revolutions are recorded by four or five small dials. Newer models have a digital readout.

Your meter is banded in place and the band is sealed by your power company. It is actually part of the service entrance circuit. When a meter is removed, the circuit is interrupted. Only when it is plugged back in can you draw electricity from the power source.

To monitor your energy consumption, note the reading at the start of the month and at the end of the month and subtract the former from the latter.

Digital electric meter

Breaker panel

How to read a meter

If your meter is an older model, it will likely have four or five dials. Each dial will be numbered from 0 to 9. As you look at these dials, you will see that they move in opposite directions. Starting from the left side, the first dial counts to the right, the second dial to the left and the third dial to the right again, and so on.

To record your meter reading, write down the numbers from each dial starting at the left. When a pointer reads between two numbers, record the lower number. When the pointer points directly to a number, look to the next dial. If the pointer to the right has reached 0, or has passed 0, write down the number indicated by the pointer at the left. Repeat this process until you have a number for each dial. That figure will give you the exact number of kilowatt-hours consumed. To determine how much electricity you use in a month, read the meter at the beginning of the month and again at the end of the month.

Fuse panel

Reading a meter: The reading indicated here would be 76579.

The service entrance panel

From the meter, your service wires enter your home either through the roof or through a wall. (Thirty-amp services usually have one black and one white wire, while 60- to 100-amp or greater services usually have two black wires and one white wire.) Service wires are usually encased in metal or plastic conduit from the weather head to the service panel. Once inside the panel, the two hot (black) wires attach to a main switch, or disconnect. The neutral (white) wire is attached to the neutral bus bar. At this point, a ground wire, usually bare No. 6 copper, is connected to the bus bar as well and then fastened to a copper grounding rod or metal plumbing pipes or both. (Some panels have separate neutral and ground bus bars, which are bonded together in the panels.)

How your home's wiring connects to the service panel depends upon the age of the system and whether or not subpanels are used. An older home may have a main panel with a disconnect switch, a bus bar, and a ground conductor. In this case, the panel serves only as a distribution box and a main disconnect. From the main panel, one black positive and one red positive wire (the NEC no longer requires one hot conductor to be coded red), together with a white neutral wire and a green ground, travel to one or more subpanels where the positive wires are connected to "hot" bus bars and neutral wires are connected to neutral bus bars. Older homes may also be wired directly to a main panel, without subpanels. In this case, each circuit would have its own fuse in the main panel.

A new home is likely to have a panel with built-in breakers. In this case, subpanels are not generally used. All the circuits are connected to a "hot" bus bar through snap-in, or slide-in, breakers. In this configuration, the positive wire of every 120-volt circuit will be attached to the breaker and the neutral and ground wires will be connected to the neutral bus bar. The 240-volt circuits will be similarly wired, except that two positive wires will be attached to each breaker. Once the panel is wired, connecting breakers and new circuits is relatively simple.

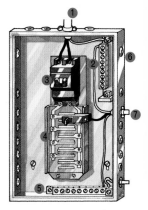
Main components of a typical service panel
1 Power supply from meter
2 Neutral bus
3 Main disconnect
4 Hot bus
5 Ground bus
6 Knockout
7 Cable to house circuit

Breakers and fuses

20-amp Edison-base fuse

Fuses and breakers are safety buffers that keep an electrical malfunction from starting a fire. A fuse can blow or a breaker trip when one of three things happens. The most frequent cause is an overloaded circuit. When too many lights or appliances are plugged into a circuit, they call for more amperage than the circuit can deliver. This amperage overload causes the conductors or wires to heat up, which causes the fuses to blow. A short circuit will also cause a fuse to blow because of the greatly increased electrical charge it sends through the circuit. And finally, a fuse will blow when it is loose in its socket. This last cause is easy to fix, but the other two are not always so easy. It is crucial to determine what may be causing a fuse to blow or a breaker to trip repeatedly.

Types of fuses

Edison-base fuses

A traditional Edison-base fuse contains a thin metal strip or wire that melts when a circuit heats up excessively. When the strip melts, it separates and interrupts the flow of electrons. The glass and ceramic housing encasing the strip keeps the molten metal from escaping and becoming a fire hazard.

The glass window on the front of an Edison-base fuse allows you to see if the strip is intact. When the fuse blows, the window also offers some clues in tracking down the source of the problem. If the window is blackened by carbon, the cause of the overload is probably a short circuit.

A short creates heat quickly and burns the fuse at high temperature, which smokes the glass. If the glass is clear and you can see the melted strip, the circuit probably heated up more slowly, indicating an amperage overload.

If a newly installed

Edison-base fuse blows as well, notice how long it took to blow. If it blew immediately, assume a short circuit. Often the culprit is an appliance, most likely its cord or plug. The only remedy is to fix the appliance and install a new fuse.

If a single circuit blows often but with no evident pattern, assume an overload. Unplug one or more lamps or appliances until a new circuit can be added.

Time-delay fuses

Some heavy tools and electric motors require three times as much amperage for startup as they need for running. If a fuse blows only when you start an electric shop tool or a window air conditioner, you can circumvent the startup overload by installing a time-delay Edison-base fuse. If the fuse blows, unplug a few lamps or appliances or quit using the tool until you can add a new circuit.

Type-S fuses

Don't be tempted to install 20-amp fuses in 15-amp sockets. If an overloaded fuse can't overheat, the wiring in your home

will, and overheated wires cause fires. If you move into an older home, check to see that the previous owner has not upsized a fuse. To further protect yourself, install nontamperable Type-S fuses. These fuses come with variously sized threaded adapters that screw into universal panel sockets. Once installed, they cannot be removed. From then on, only 15-amp Type-S fuses can be used for this circuit.

Cartridge-type fuses

Cartridge fuses can be found in many older homes and are often used as main panel fuses. They may also be used to protect subpanels, but the most common installation has two cartridge fuses at the main disconnect.

Ferrule-type cartridges can be rated between 10 and 60 amps and are frequently used in subpanels and on branch circuits or appliance circuits. Knife-blade cartridges snap into service panel clips. Because they are rated higher than 60 amps, they are often used as main panel protectors.

Breakers

Breakers have replaced fuses almost entirely in the last 25 years. Unlike a blown fuse, a tripped breaker does not have to be replaced. When a short or overload trips a breaker, all you need to do is turn it back on. In addition to being a perpetually renewable circuit protector, a breaker can withstand the temporary amperage surges often created when electric motors first start up. So, in a sense, a breaker has a built-in time-delay feature. You can also buy Edison-base replacement breakers that screw directly

into older service panels. To reactivate these breakers, you simply push a small button in the center of the breaker.

Breakers differ slightly in appearance and operation from one manufacturer to another. The main difference is that some breaker switches do not return to the off position when tripped. You will have to shut them off all the way before flipping them on again. Breakers also differ in how they snap into panels. You will have to buy breakers to match the brand name on your service panel.

Edison-base replacement breakers
By pushing button, power is restored

Renewable breakers
Modern panels use renewable breakers

Two things determine the expansion capabilities of your home's electrical system. Most important is the maximum amp rating of your service entrance. The other is the amount of circuit space left—if any—in your service panel.

Mapping your home's wiring

Before you can know how much expansion your 60-amp system will safely handle, you will need to determine how much amperage each circuit is using. The best way to do this is to make a map of your home's circuitry. This isn't as difficult as it sounds. All you need is a floor-plan drawing of your home, a voltage tester or lamp, and a little deductive reasoning.

Making the map

Start by drawing the perimeter of your home on graph paper. Use a simple ⅛-inch-to-1-foot scale (i.e., each square on the graph paper equals 1 square foot of living space). Then draw the approximate location of all interior walls. If you have a two- or three-story house, make a drawing for each floor. If you have a basement, lighted patio, or deck and a wired garage or other outbuilding, draw them too. Then indicate the location of outlet boxes and permanent light fixtures.

Start by removing the fuse or tripping the breaker on the first circuit in the panel. Mark that breaker or fuse No. 1. Then take your voltage tester or small lamp and plug it into all outlets near the circuit you've just interrupted. Next to each outlet on the map that doesn't work, place the number 1. Then go back to the service panel, restore power to the circuit you've just checked, and shut off the power to the next circuit in the panel. Be sure to number each fuse or breaker in the panel as you go.

With power to the second circuit shut off, locate and number all fixtures and outlets on the map that do not work. Do this with each circuit until you have isolated each circuit and determined how many outlets and fixtures are served by each. Also check and mark down your major appliances, such as a range, water heater, or clothes dryer that have dedicated 240-volt circuits. When you are done, every outlet and fixture should have a number. Tape the map to the inside of the panel cover for future reference.

Rating your panel

To determine what rating your service panel has, open the panel cover and look for the amperage designation near the main disconnect. If your service and panel are rated at 100 amps or more, you are in luck. If it is rated at 60 amps or less, expansion will be limited. If your needs require a substantial upgrade, consider having a larger service and panel installed by a licensed electrician.

Your ability to install new circuits depends on the number of breaker or fuse spaces left in the panel. A home's wiring doesn't always need all the breaker slots in a 100-amp or greater panel. If you see vacant slots, an expansion will be easy. Each slot will hold one new 15- or 20-amp circuit. If you have two vacant slots, your panel will accommodate a new 240-volt circuit.

If yours is an older 60-amp panel, however, all available fuse spaces will likely be taken. A 60-amp service panel will also limit the number of 240-volt appliance outlets you can have. One 240-volt and four 120-volt circuits is the limit in 60-amp panels. If your 60-amp panel has the room and the available amperage, wiring a new circuit will be as easy as wiring from a new breaker. If the panel is full, but you have two underrated circuits, you can sometimes combine the two and free one circuit for expansion.

Determining total amperage
Each permanent light and outlet should be rated at 1.5 amps. This means that a 15-amp fuse or breaker (on No. 14 wire) will support 10 outlets. A 20-amp fuse or breaker (on No. 12 wire) will support 13 outlets. If your mapping identifies a circuit that can support additional outlets, you can tap into that circuit at any location to add new outlets.

If your map identifies two circuits with so few outlets that both circuits could be protected by a single fuse, you can combine those two circuits in the panel, thus freeing one whole circuit for expansion.

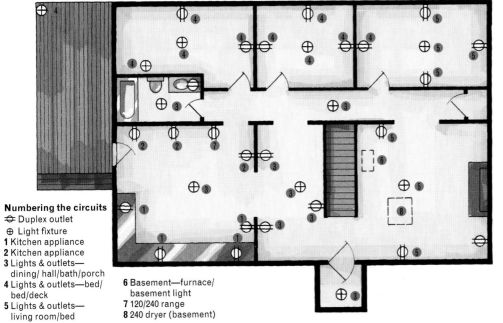

Numbering the circuits
⊖ Duplex outlet
⊕ Light fixture
1 Kitchen appliance
2 Kitchen appliance
3 Lights & outlets—
 dining/ hall/bath/porch
4 Lights & outlets—bed/
 bed/deck
5 Lights & outlets—
 living room/bed
6 Basement—furnace/
 basement light
7 120/240 range
8 240 dryer (basement)

Electrical fittings and fixtures

Once you decide to tackle a project, you'll have to shop for materials, and here's where things can get confusing. There's a wide variety of electrical hardware out there and it's not always easy to know what goes where. Here are some of the most common items with a brief description of what each one is commonly used for and why.

Electrical tape

All electrical connections must be housed in closed electrical boxes. Boxes also hold switches, lights, and receptacles securely in place. You'll find several different shapes in plastic and metal and each type has a specific use.

Weatherproof box is designed for outdoor use and, when fitted with the correct coverplate, is watertight.

Cut-in box is used for retrofit work. You just cut a hole in the wall and slide the box in. The side flanges hold it in place.

Handy box is made for external mounting and is used with armored cable or conduit.

Two-gang box has space for two receptacles, two switches, or one of each.

Grounding pigtail
This allows you to join ground wires together with a wire connector on the bare end, and then to attach them to the back of a metal box with the grounding screw on the other end.

Switch box is designed for one switch, but the sides can be removed so it can be ganged with other switch boxes.

The most common receptacles are the duplex variety for 15- and 20-amp circuits. Most come with screw terminals and push-in slots for attaching wires. A more specialized model is the GFCI (ground fault circuit interrupter) receptacle. It's used in damp or wet areas to protect you from dangerous short circuits.

Switches may be single pole, for turning off power to a fixture from one location, or three-way, for switching power from two locations. But not all lights are switched remotely. Some have a pull-chain switch built in, like the keyed light fixture at right.

Various coverplates round out this selection of basic hardware. They're available in different sizes, configurations, and colors.

Cable connectors
Conduit connector (top) attaches conduit to box. Cable connector (above) joins cable to box.

Weatherproof box   Cut-in box   Handy box

2-gang box   Switch box

15-amp duplex receptacle   20-amp duplex receptacle   GFCI receptacle

Single-pole switch   Three-way switch   Keyed light fixture

Coverplates

Wire basics

Most electrical wiring today is made of copper. Copper is a good conductor and is flexible enough to handle twists and turns without breaking. Because circuit wires (conductors) will create a short circuit if they touch, they are usually encased in plastic insulation. As all circuits require two or more conductors, electrical supply makers offer two or more conductors in a single plastic or nonmetallic sleeve. Wire in this form is called cable. Individual conductors that go from one location to another without being part of a cable must be encased in rigid or flexible conduit.

Electrical wire is sized by gauge number, from the smallest size, No. 18, to the largest residential size, No. 1. Wire size is a critical factor in a home's wiring system. Just as a small pipe size can carry only so many gallons of water, small conductors can carry only so many amperes. When a wire is forced to carry more amperes than it can handle, resistance increases and the wire heats up. As a wire heats up, it either blows a fuse or becomes a fire hazard. When you do any wiring project, make sure to follow NEC specifications. This sizing guide will help you choose the right wire size for each project.

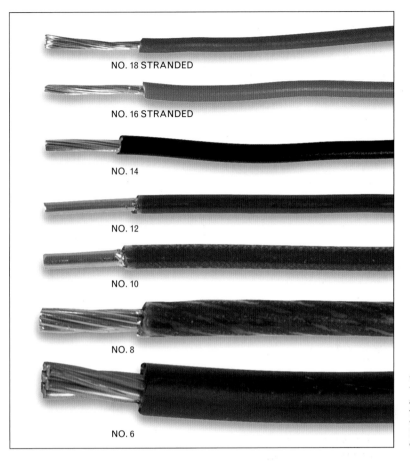

NO. 18 STRANDED

NO. 16 STRANDED

NO. 14

NO. 12

NO. 10

NO. 8

NO. 6

Wire types and uses
The wire sizes used in a typical home range from No. 18 stranded wire for doorbells to No. 6 wire for service conductors.

RESIDENTIAL WIRE SIZING GUIDE

Wire size	Common use	Amps
No. 18	Low voltage (LV)	7
No. 16	LV/doorbells	10
No. 14	Lights, outlets	15
No. 12	Small appliances/ 120 volt	20
No. 10	Large appliance/ 120 volt	30
No. 8	Larger appliance/ 120 volt	40
No. 6	Single appliance/ 240 volt	55
No. 4	Single appliance/ 240 volt	70

Identify wires by color

To give electrical wiring an instantly recognizable standard in the field, the NEC has designated an insulation color for each conductor function. A black wire, for example, is always the "hot," or positive, side of a circuit. A red wire is also positive. If you see a black wire and a red wire in the same cable, you know that circuit has two hot wires and is therefore usually a 240-volt circuit. A white wire is always neutral, unless used as a traveler on a three-way switch. In that case, the white insulation should be marked with black paint or black tape to distinguish it from the white neutral in the same box. Blue wires can also be hot when substituted for black in conduit. Green and yellow are always ground wires, as is bare copper wire. While these designators are excellent indicators, don't trust your life to them. The homeowner before you may have invented his own coding system. Protect yourself from nonconformists by testing each circuit you work on with a voltage tester before starting the job.

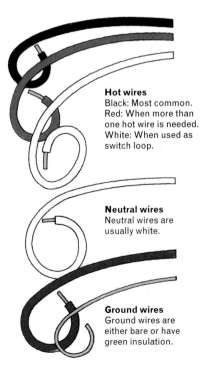

Hot wires
Black: Most common.
Red: When more than one hot wire is needed.
White: When used as switch loop.

Neutral wires
Neutral wires are usually white.

Ground wires
Ground wires are either bare or have green insulation.

Cable types and uses

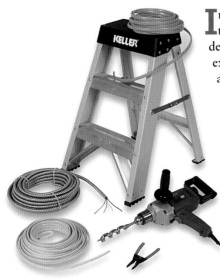

In the field, the terms wire and cable are often used interchangeably. To be exact, however, the term "wire" refers to a single conductor, insulated or uninsulated. The term "cable" is used to describe several wires encased in a single sleeve or sheath—12/2 cable with ground, for example, contains two insulated No. 12 wires and one paper-wrapped ground wire. This same arrangement of wires might also be run as single strands inside of conduit, but in this case would not be called cable. And because the ground wire would not have the protection of a plastic sleeve, as in an insulated cable, it would need to be an insulated wire.

Types of wire

Type T wire is most commonly used in residential installations where conduit is used. It has a tough insulation, called thermoplastic, that will accommodate both hot and cold weather extremes. Type TW is a designation for all-weather installations and can be used in aboveground outdoor installations. It has a slightly heavier plastic coating that provides more protection from temperature extremes and moisture.

Types of cable

Because residential wiring is simpler than commercial wiring and requires fewer provisions for change, cable is used instead of conduit and wire. A variety of cable types have been developed to meet a variety of special needs. In most cases, the job will dictate the cable type you use.

NM cable is the most commonly used in residential systems. It is made of two or more type T wires and a bare-wire ground, all encased in a plastic sleeve. The ground wire is wrapped in paper and is positioned between the two insulated wires. The paper wrap makes this type of cable unsuitable for damp situations.

NMC cable is specifically designed for damp situations. Instead of paper wrap, all three wires are encased in a solid plastic strip. NMC is often used in basement installations.

UF cable is designed to be used in underground installations of outdoor lighting and as a lateral cable to outbuildings. It too is encased in plastic and is moistureproof.

A last category, armored cable or BX, is rarely used today but must be reckoned with in older homes. It was designed to be used where ordinary cable might be punctured by nails. The distinguishing feature of armored cable is that the metal armor itself helps to ground the circuit it serves. Armored cable is harder to work with than NM or UF. This is one reason why it is used almost exclusively in commercial and industrial situations.

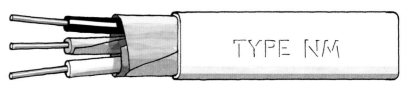

Type NM, three-wire with ground

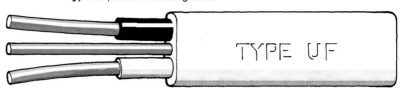

Type UF waterproof cable

Armored cable

In the early fifties, manufacturers looking for a less expensive conductor introduced aluminum wire to the market. The industry soon learned, however, that aluminum wire came with some very serious problems.

It is not as efficient a conductor as copper and therefore offers more resistance to current. As the wire heats up, it expands, and repeated expansion and contraction eventually cause the wires to loosen under terminal screws. The short circuits that occur in the process regularly trip breakers and can cause fires. A compromise wire was also manufactured. It too was made of aluminum but was clad in copper. Copper-clad wire is allowed by some code authorities, but not by others.

To protect yourself against the problems caused by aluminum wire, it's best to replace all switches and receptacles with ones made to accommodate aluminum. If your switches and receptacles have no designation markings, don't use them. Use only those with "CO/ALR" (approved for copper and aluminum wire) designations.

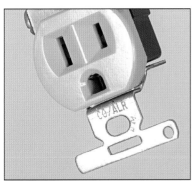

Aluminum wiring requires receptacles and switches designated CO/ALR.

Working with wire does not require a large investment in tools. In fact, you can do a lot with needle-nose pliers and a sharp pocket knife. If you do more than replace an occasional receptacle, however, you should consider investing in a few wireworking tools. Your first purchase should be a multipurpose tool, pliers that cut and strip many different sizes of wire. A sharp utility knife is also a big help. Needle-nose pliers are a must, as are sturdy side cutter pliers. Add a Phillips and flat-blade screwdriver and you should have all you need for just about every job.

Stripping wire

You can buy a sheathing stripper, but a sharp knife works just as well if you are careful **(1)**. Because the uninsulated ground wire runs through the center of the sheathing, make your cut in the middle of one side. Make the cut shallow to avoid nicking the insulated wires. Then pull the split sheathing back from the wires and cut it off **(2)**.

With the sheathing gone, strip approximately ½ inch of insulation from each insulated wire. You can use a knife, but a multipurpose tool works better. In any case, avoid cutting into the copper. Slide the end of the wire into the correct numbered slot in the handle of the tool **(3)**, then squeeze, twist, and pull **(4)**. If you have the wire in the right hole, the insulation will strip right off the wire and won't nick the copper in the process.

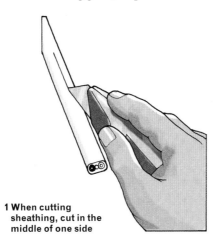

1 When cutting sheathing, cut in the middle of one side

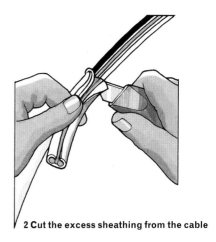

2 Cut the excess sheathing from the cable

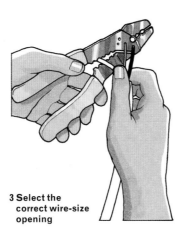

3 Select the correct wire-size opening

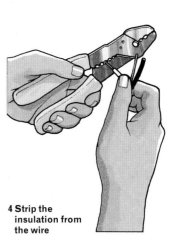

4 Strip the insulation from the wire

Splicing wires

Wire connections, no matter where they are made, must be very tight. Loose connections will only get looser over time and in the process will create resistance, which in turn creates heat. Hot connections trip breakers and if they are allowed to spark, can cause fires.

Connecting solid wires

To join two solid wires, strip ½ inch of insulation from each wire and twist the stripped wires together with pliers in a clockwise direction. Then select a wire connector large enough to slide over the twisted wires about half way. Insert the wires into the connector and turn it until the wire is drawn in and the connector no longer turns. The more wires you join, the larger the connector you will need. Make sure that no copper shows outside the connector. If it does, take off the connector, trim the wires to length with side cutter pliers, and reinstall the connector.

Join solid wires with wire connector.

Stranded wire connections

When connecting stranded wire, strip about ½ inch of insulation from each wire and twist the strands together in a clockwise direction until no loose ends can be seen. Then turn the connector on until it is tight.

When connecting stranded wire to solid wire, strip ½ inch of insulation from the solid wire and about ¾ inch from the stranded wire. Wrap the stranded wire tightly around the solid wire in a clockwise direction. Then tighten a connector over them.

When connecting wires to switch or receptacle terminals, strip about ⅝ inch of insulation from each wire, then use needle-nose pliers to form a small loop or hook. Loosen the terminal screw until the loop fits under the screw clockwise. Then tighten the screw. Because receptacle terminals can hold only one wire, and because code now requires it, use a pigtail connection from the receptacle to the circuit wires.

When connecting to a push-in switch or receptacle with self-locking slots, strip only ½ inch of insulation from the wires and push each into the back of the device until no copper can be seen. If any copper remains exposed, depress the locking clip next to the slot and pull the wire out. Then clip the end of the wire and push it back in.

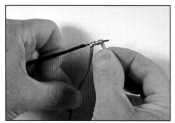

Wrap stranded wire around solid wire.

Install pigtails on receptacle terminals.

Strip wire and slide into push-in terminals.

Continuity testers

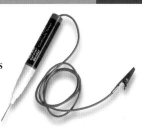

Continuity testers allow you to test across conductors without having the power on, which makes them ideal for testing appliance switches and connections. Unlike voltage testers, continuity testers have their own battery-supplied power. The light in a continuity tester comes on when its circuit is completed by a switch, conductor, or appliance. It is important to turn off power to any circuit or part before testing it with a continuity tester, as house current will blow the tester bulb.

Testing fuses

To see if a fuse is still working, touch the probe of the tester to the metal threads of the fuse and the tester's alligator clip to the contact at the base of the fuse. If the fuse is good, the light in the tester's handle will glow.

To test a cartridge fuse, simply touch the probe to one end and the clip to the other. If the fuse completes the circuit and lights the bulb, it's good.

Test Edison fuse on threads and contact point

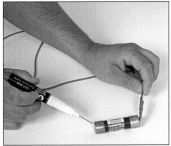

Test cartridge fuse at both ends

Testing toggle switches

When testing any switch with a continuity tester, shut off the power and remove the switch completely. To test a single-pole switch, place the alligator clip on one terminal and touch the probe to the other. When the switch is in the on position, the tester should light up.

To test three-way switches, determine which of the three terminal screws is the "common" terminal. Some manufacturers identify the common terminal by labeling it, while others color the common screw black or brass. The traveler screws will be bright silver. Place the alligator clip on the common screw and touch the probe to one of the other terminals. Flip the switch one way and the tester light should go on. Then touch the probe to the other terminal; the tester light should go on this time when the switch is in the opposite position.

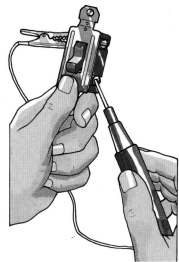

Testing a switch
In the case of this three-way switch, both toggle positions should be tested.

Testing lamp switches

To test a lamp switch, unplug the lamp and fasten the alligator clip to the brass-colored terminal screw and touch the probe to the contact tab inside the socket. When you turn the switch on, the light in the tester should glow. If it does not, replace the switch.

Testing three-way lamp switches
A three-way lamp switch has three opportunities to malfunction because it has three separate circuits inside the device. If you have a lamp with a three-way switch that is giving you trouble, unplug the cord and remove the switch. Then attach the alligator clip to the brass screw terminal. (The other terminal will be colored bright silver.)

Turn the switch to the first "on" position. When you touch the probe to the small vertical tab in the base, the tester light should come on. Then turn to the second on position. Touch the probe to the round center tab and the tester light should come on.

Finally, turn the lamp to the third on position. If the tester light comes on when you touch both tabs simultaneously, the switch is not defective. You will probably find the problem in the cord or the plug. (If you can't get the probe to touch both tabs at the same time, use the clip end of the tester to touch the tabs and use the probe end of the tester to touch the terminal screw.) If the tester fails to light in any one of the three on positions, replace the switch.

Testing a lamp switch
With the alligator clip clamped to the socket threads, touch the probe to the silver screw.

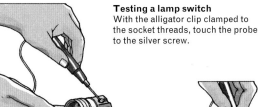

Testing a three-way lamp switch
Touch the probe to the vertical tab, the rounded tab, and finally, both tabs at once.

Voltage testers

Testing receptacle
Slide one tester probe into each slot.

Testing for hot wire
Place one probe on black wire, the other on metal box.

Checking grounding
If the box or receptacle is grounded, the light will come on brightly. A dim light suggests a poor ground wire connection.

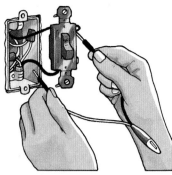

Testing switch
To check if switch is hot, place one probe on the metal box, the other on a screw terminal.

A voltage tester is a simple, inexpensive device that tells you if there is electricity in a cable, outlet, or switch. A voltage tester has no power of its own, but merely conducts voltage from one wire to another. As current passes through the wires, it lights a small neon bulb, which signals the presence of a current. Because a voltage tester can keep you from inadvertently touching a hot wire, you should buy one before you begin any wiring project. Voltage testers are also useful in testing your work for proper grounding and for determining which wire in a cable is hot.

Testing a receptacle

To see if a receptacle is working, insert one wire of the tester into each plug slot. If the tester light comes on, the receptacle is energized. If not, the receptacle is defective or a fuse has blown. To determine if the problem is in one receptacle only, test the other receptacles on the circuit. If none works, the problem is in the circuit. If only one receptacle is defective, shut off the power to the entire circuit at the panel and test again to make sure the circuit is off, then replace the defective receptacle.

Locating the hot wire in a cable

When working in a switch, receptacle, or light fixture box that contains two or more black wires, you will need to determine which black wire is hot. It is always possible that someone before you wired the white wire hot instead of the black wire, which can be confusing.

To find which wire is hot, separate the wires at the box so that they cannot make contact with each other. Then touch one tester probe to the metal box and the other to each of the black wires. The one that lights the tester bulb is the incoming hot wire. For future reference, you may wish to mark that wire with a piece of tape. If you are working inside a plastic outlet box, you will not be able to test the ground against the box. Instead, touch one probe to the bare ground wire in the box and the other to one of the black wires.

Checking for proper grounding

Properly grounded receptacles are very important to the safety of your electrical system. Use your voltage tester to make sure every receptacle is grounded well. Insert one tester probe into the hot slot of the receptacle and touch the other probe to the coverplate screw. (The hot slot on newer receptacles is the smaller of the two. If the coverplate screw is painted, chip some paint from its head or turn the screw out far enough to reach the unpainted threads.) If the receptacle is a three-prong model, insert the ground probe into the U-shaped ground slot. The tester light should burn brightly. If the light seems weak, check for a poor ground wire connection.

Testing a switch

To determine whether a switch is hot, remove the coverplate and touch one probe of your tester to the metal box or bare ground wire. Then touch the other probe to each of the wired terminals. If the light burns from each of these terminals, the switch is hot. If the switch is hot, shut the power off in the panel before working on the switch or the circuit.

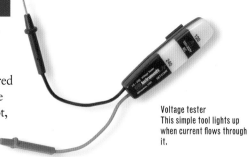

Voltage tester
This simple tool lights up when current flows through it.

Dealing with electric shock

Severe electric shock can arrest the heart and interrupt the victim's breathing. Often, when someone is exposed to an electrical short, he or she will not be able to let go. If you see this happen, use a towel or any poor conductor to pull the person free. If nothing else is available, try to knock the person loose with a kick or a push. Do not grab and maintain contact for more than a split second. You too will become part of the short circuit and will be unable to let go. The longer a person is in contact with a short, the more damage is done.

Isolate the victim from the short circuit

First-aid kit
Always have a well-stocked first-aid kit around the house to help with any injuries.

Clear away obstructions

Open the airway

Unless the victim's airway is opened, air cannot enter the lungs. If the victim is not breathing, the airway may be blocked. Clear the mouth of obstructions (food, gum, objects). Lay the victim on his or her back and tilt the head back by placing your hand on the forehead and lifting the chin up with your other hand. This keeps the tongue from blocking the airway.

Check for breathing

Once the airway is open, check for signs of breathing. Look to see if the victim's chest is rising and falling, listen for air being exhaled, and feel with your cheek and ear for air escaping through the victim's nose and mouth. If the victim is not breathing, you should begin rescue breathing.

Mouth-to-mouth

Keeping his head tilted back with one hand on the forehead, pinch the victim's nostrils shut with your thumb and forefinger. Take a deep breath and cover the victim's mouth with your own, making a seal. Blow deeply and slowly into the mouth, watching to see if the chest is rising and falling. Ventilate the victim's lungs two times with slow, full breaths. After the first two full breaths, continue giving one breath every five seconds for as long as you can. Check the victim often to see if breathing has begun.

Mouth-to-nose

If the victim's mouth is burned for any reason, you might breathe through the nose. Keeping the head tilted back, push the victim's mouth closed with your free hand. Place your mouth over the nose while sealing the mouth with your cheek. Proceed as you would for mouth-to-mouth.

Reviving a child

If the victim is a baby or small child, cover both the nose and the mouth with your mouth, then proceed as above, but use gentle puffs of air.

Breathe into a child's mouth and nose

Recovery

Once the victim starts breathing, place him or her in a semi-prone position. Observe carefully to see if the breathing continues regularly. Keep the victim warm with blankets until medical help arrives.

Tilt head back to open airway

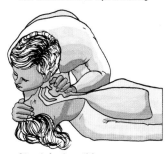

Check for breathing

Breathe into the victim's airway

Repairing cords and plugs

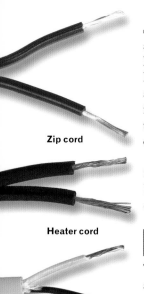

Zip cord

Heater cord

Vacuum cleaner cord

Power cord

A variety of cord types are used to supply lamps, power tools, portable heaters, and small appliances. These cords usually consist of No. 16 or No. 18 stranded wire covered by two or three thin layers of paper insulation and plastic. The wire strands and the minimal insulation allow flex cords to be flexible. But over time, the insulation breaks down and the protective covering wears thin. When bare wires are exposed, a short circuit can occur.

Years of use can threaten plugs as well. Plugs frequently tear loose, and rough handling can also break a plug's housing, which can cause a short to occur between the prongs.

Replacing plugs

To replace a faulty plug, cut the cord several inches away from the plug. Then separate the two wires for about 3 inches and strip ⅝ inch of insulation from each wire. Take the cover off the new plug prongs. Then feed the separated and stripped cord into the plug housing. Tie the two wires and fasten them to the terminals. Then replace the prong cover.

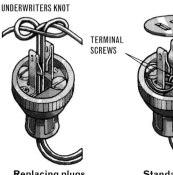

UNDERWRITERS KNOT

TERMINAL SCREWS

ZIP CORD

CONTACTS

PLUG HOUSING

Self-piercing plug
Each half pierces the cord, making contact.

Replacing plugs
Tie the two wires inside the plug.

Standard plug
Make sure stranded wires are twisted.

Replacing a lamp socket

Lamp sockets tend to wear out sooner than other components. Luckily, they are inexpensive and easy to replace. First, unplug the cord and remove the lamp shade and bulb. Then find the place on the socket marked "press." Press firmly against the socket and the components will separate. Once apart, remove all components and thread the new socket base onto the threaded nipple with the wires pulled through the new base. Tie the two wires together and connect them to their respective terminals. Finally, replace the brass shell, bulb, and shade.

Replacing cords

You can buy replacement flex cords by the foot or in precut lengths that have plugs already on them. In the case of electric irons, replacement cords even have protective rubber sleeves on the appliance end to keep them from bending too sharply and breaking. The type you buy will depend mostly on the appliance and the appliance's proximity to a wall outlet.

Regardless of which cord you buy, the appliance end is a pretty simple hookup. In many cases, you will have to take the appliance apart, usually by loosening several screws in the housing. Some appliances have access panels that make connecting the cord easier. Many lamps have felt or cardboard base covers that can be pried loose. In any case, let the old cord be your guide to installing a new one. You can even tie the new cord to the old one and pull it through.

Once you've brought the cord into the lamp or appliance, you will find two or three wire terminals, or in some cases, color-coded lead wires. If you find terminals, strip approximately ⅝ inch of insulation from the end of the wires. Twist the stranded wire and bend it into a clockwise hook. Lay the hook under the terminals and tighten them down. In most cases, two-wire cords cannot be cross-wired. If the cord wires are not color coded, don't worry about which terminal gets a given wire.

If you find two lead wires instead of terminals, you will have to join the new cord to the appliance leads with plastic solderless connectors. If your new cord has three wires, join the leads as usual and fasten the third grounding wire (usually green) to the grounding terminal inside the appliance.

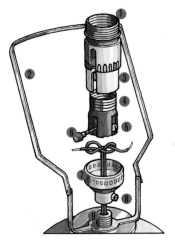

The components of a typical lamp
1 Socket shell
2 Harp
3 Insulating sleeve
4 Socket
5 Terminal screw
6 Switch
7 Socket cap
8 Set screw
9 Threaded nipple

Incandescent fixtures

Ceiling or wall-mounted light fixtures can be expected to last a long time. Even when they appear to be defective, often the problem can be traced to wall switches or the wiring between the switch and fixture. Light fixtures, therefore, are usually replaced for reasons of style or because they don't have the bulb capacity to provide adequate light. When shopping for a new fixture, make sure it can deliver the amount of light you need and try to find one that has a cover, or canopy, as large as the one on your existing fixture. A smaller canopy may require some touch-up painting or even some drywall or plaster repair.

Whatever the reason for replacing a light fixture, you'll be glad to know that the project is a simple one because all fixtures, regardless of outward appearance, have similar internal parts. And because the switch for the fixture is already in place, you don't have a lot of retrofit wiring to do. Also, nearly all fixtures (whether mounted on the wall or the ceiling) are fastened to ceiling outlet boxes, which makes the fixture-to-box connection nearly universal.

Installing a new fixture

To install a new fixture, start by fastening the strap to the box. If your fixture requires a threaded nipple, turn it into the strap. Then, hold the fixture up to the box so that the fixture lead wires can be attached to the switch wires in the box. Hold each color-matched set of wires together and tighten a wire connector over them. No bare wire should be showing when the connectors are in place. With the switch wires connected to the lead wires, fasten the canopy either to the strap with the mounting screws or to the threaded nipple with a nut. Install the globe, or diffuser as it's often called, to the fixture. For standard strap mount fixtures, the diffuser is held by three screws mounted in the rim of the canopy. For threaded-nipple fixtures, the diffuser is held by a nut threaded onto the end of the nipple.

One word of caution is in order when it comes to ceiling fixtures, especially those with closed diffusers: Never install a bulb with a higher wattage rating than the fixture is designed to hold. Bulbs of higher wattage can overheat the socket wiring. Hot fixtures can start fires. You will find the recommended watt rating stamped somewhere on the fixture.

Removing a light fixture

To remove an old ceiling or wall fixture, start by shutting the power off at the panel. Then loosen the set screws or center nut that holds the glass diffuser to the fixture body. With the diffuser off, undo the center nut or canopy screws from the decorative cover or canopy. Pull the canopy down to expose the wires and the mounting strap. Then remove the strap from the box and pull the wires out. Separate the wire connections or remove the wire connectors and the fixture will come free.

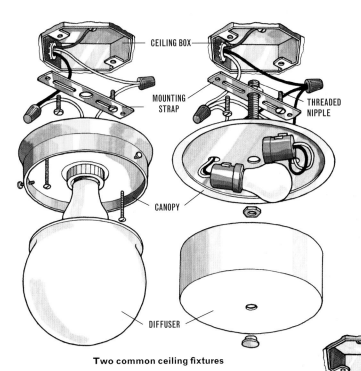

CEILING BOX

MOUNTING STRAP

THREADED NIPPLE

CANOPY

DIFFUSER

Two common ceiling fixtures

SWITCH LOOP

Wall-mounted light with receptacle

Chandelier-type fixture construction

Fluorescent fixtures

Fluorescent lights offer the best energy buy around when it comes to lighting your home. You can receive five to six times as much light from a fluorescent bulb as from an incandescent bulb of the same wattage. Fluorescent fixtures operate under a completely different principle from incandescent fixtures. When electricity is routed to a fluorescent fixture, a booster station, called a ballast, sends a surge of electricity into the fluorescent tube. Older models also include a starter to help the ballast reach maximum power in less time. This increased surge of electricity then charges gases in the bulb which in turn create a faint light. The light is then picked up and intensified by a chemical coating on the inner wall of the bulb. This three-step activation explains the familiar hesitation found in older models when first turned on. Newer models come on much faster, some almost instantly.

Installing fluorescent fixtures

Installing fluorescent fixtures is no different than installing incandescent fixtures. In both cases, the body of the fixture is held to the ceiling by a threaded nipple or screws that go into a ceiling box. Both have lead wires that are joined inside the ceiling box with wire connectors. The rest is a matter of design variation.

When replacing an incandescent fixture, shut off the electricity, undo the center nut or screws that hold the canopy in place, and remove the wire connectors from the fixture leads. Then install the new threaded nipple (if required) and strap. Hold the lamp near the box and connect the fixture leads to the switch wires. With the wires connected, slide the fixture body, called the channel, over the threaded nipple or against the strap and tighten the center nut or strap screws. Larger channels may also need to be fastened to ceiling joists with wood screws for extra support. If you have trouble finding joists, use toggle bolts or another type of hollow-cavity fastener.

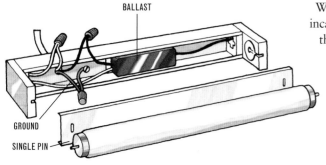

BALLAST

GROUND

SINGLE PIN

Instant-start fluorescent fixture

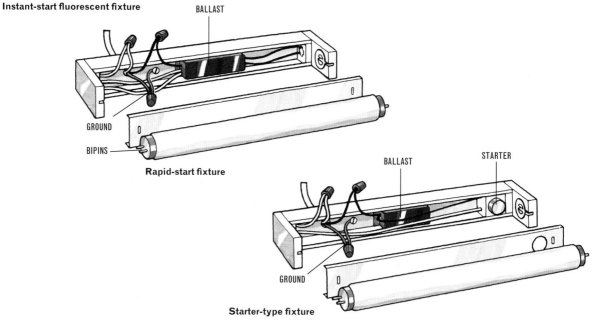

BALLAST

GROUND

BIPINS

Rapid-start fixture

BALLAST   STARTER

GROUND

Starter-type fixture

Diagnosing and repairing fluorescent fixtures

The most frequent problem you are likely to encounter with fluorescent lights is worn-out bulbs. Unlike incandescent bulbs, fluorescent tubes do not burn out abruptly. They flutter and flash on and off and act up in ways that lead homeowners to believe more serious problems exist. Don't assume the worst. Always start with the tube. If a tube will not come on at all, wiggle and twist it slightly in its sockets. Often the end pins are not seated properly.

To determine whether a troublesome tube needs to be replaced, look to the discoloration on each end. It is normal for a tube to show gray rings through the glass on each end, but when these rings turn black, the bulb needs to be replaced. Make sure that you replace it with a tube of the same wattage.

Defective starters

When older fluorescent fixtures flutter but do not come on, the problem is likely to be the starter. A starter is a small cylinder located under one of the tubes near a socket. Twist the tube out so that you can reach the starter. Then, check to see if the starter is seated properly. Push it in and try to turn it to the right. If it moves or turns to the right, replace the bulb to see if reseating the starter helped. If the light does not come on, you can assume a defective starter.

Remove the old starter by pushing in slightly and turning it a quarter-turn counterclockwise. Be sure to buy another starter with the same amp rating. Then push it into its socket and turn it to the right until it seats. Finally, replace the tube and turn the power back on. The new starter should eliminate the flickering problem immediately.

Nonstarter fixtures

Newer fluorescent fixtures come on instantly. Because of a few internal changes, starters are no longer needed. If you have trouble with one of these newer fixtures, first look to the tubes, then to the ballast, for the problem.

Replacing a ballast

The ballast is the heart of a fluorescent fixture and is therefore the most costly component to replace. In fact, if you watch the specials, you can often buy a completely new fixture for the same price as a new ballast.

A faulty ballast is characterized by a continuous buzzing sound, often accompanied by a sharp odor. To replace a ballast, shut the electricity off at the panel and remove the tubes and channel lid. Inside, you will find the ballast screwed to the channel. Clip the wires near the ballast and loosen the retaining screws that hold the ballast in place inside the fixture.

Replacement ballasts come with lead wires. Simply fasten the new ballast to the channel and join the fixture wires to the ballast leads with wire connectors. Follow the manufacturer's wiring diagram carefully to avoid joining the wrong wires together.

Unscrew the old ballast and pull it down from the channel.

Push the new ballast into place and attach it with screws.

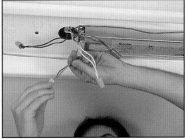

Join ballast wires to circuit wire with wire connectors.

Doorbells and thermostats

Repairing a broken doorbell may require a little detective work, but it's normally a simple enough task. The low-voltage current will do little more than tickle your fingers if you touch both wires. Not until you reach the transformer will you need to shut the power off. Everything but the wiring is surface mounted.

Testing the button

Start with the most likely culprit, the button. It gets the most use and abuse over the years. Undo the screws that hold the button to the house trim and locate the wires. Remove one of the two thin wires from its terminal and touch it to the other wire or terminal. If the bell rings, you probably need a new button. Simply attach the two existing wires to the terminals of the new button and fasten the new button to the door trim or house siding. Some buttons fasten directly, others have baseplates. Low voltage requires no ground wire.

Repairing broken wires

As you work your way through the system, carefully check for loose connections, broken wires, or frayed insulation. If you find broken wires, splice them with small wire connectors and tape. If you find frayed insulation, tape each wire individually near the problem area. And of course, restore any loose connections you find.

Cleaning clapper and bell

If, when someone rings your doorbell, you hear a muffled buzz instead of the bell, suspect a dirty or gummed-up clapper contact. Remove the cover and clean the clapper contact thoroughly. If it does not respond at all to an electrical charge, you probably need a new one. First, remove the old cover, bell, and wall bracket. To keep the wires from falling into the wall space, pull them out as far as you can and guide them through the opening of a new wall bracket. Then screw the new bracket to the wall so that it is level. Connect the existing wires to the new terminals and snap the cover over the bell or chime mechanism.

Unscrew the doorbell button from the side of the house.

Tape the wires to the house so they won't fall into the hole.

Connect wires to back of new button and screw to the house.

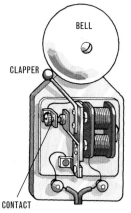
A typical clapper-type doorbell

Checking the transformer

If the bell does not ring when you test the button, look to the transformer. The transformer will be attached to the side of a 120-volt junction box, usually in the basement. To determine if the transformer is working, undo the two low-voltage wires and use a screwdriver to arc across the terminals. Lay the screwdriver on one terminal and lightly touch it to the other terminal. If you see a tiny spark, the transformer is sending current through the lines.

If no spark is produced, assume a faulty transformer. Shut off the power that serves the transformer outlet. Then remove the screws that hold the old transformer to the box. Attach the leads from the new transformer to the 120-volt conductors inside the box and mount the new transformer on the outlet cover. Install the outlet cover, attach the low-voltage wires to the transformer terminals, and restore power to the circuit.

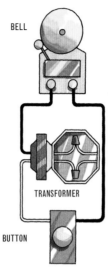

A typical doorbell loop

Replacing a thermostat

Replacing a thermostat is an easy job when you buy the right replacement. Before shopping for a new one, pry the cover off of your current thermostat and check to see how many wires come through the wall. Furnaces without air conditioning will require only two wires, while furnaces with air conditioning require four and sometimes five wires. Make sure that the thermostat you choose is compatible with your existing system. Look for a brand name and model number and try for an exact replacement.

Start by removing the cover from the old thermostat. This will expose the wires and the heat-sensitive switch. Disconnect the wires, but make sure you note how they were hooked up. Then remove the screws holding the baseplate to the wall. Be careful not to let the wires fall behind the wall finish into the stud space.

Then slide the wires through the new baseplate and fasten it to the wall. Make sure that the baseplate is perfectly level, or the mercury switch may give you a false temperature reading. With the base installed, connect the wires to the terminal according to the manufacturer's instructions.

To replace an old thermostat, begin by removing the thermostat cover.

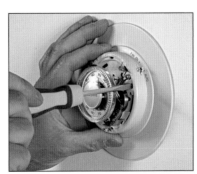

Find the screws that attach the thermostat to its baseplate and remove them.

Grounding the system

Ground faults

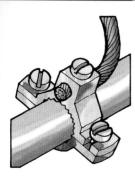

You can always expect electricity to find the path of least resistance. Current will flow through a larger wire before a smaller one, through copper more readily than aluminum or iron. Given a choice, electricity would rather flow through copper than almost anything else, including a human body. This fact is the basis of all grounding. As long as we provide an easier grounding conductor, such as copper, we are kept from becoming conductors ourselves.

The electrical current in your home's system starts its circular flow at the main breaker, through the black wire. After it passes through a fixture, it travels back to the panel through the white wire. A copper gounding wire runs in the same cable. In the service panel all the individual grounding wires are joined to a large one that runs outside the house and is attached to a copper rod driven into the ground. This large wire becomes the path of least resistance, should current become sidetracked. It will carry any dangerous current to the ground, where it will dissipate, hence the term "grounding."

Short circuits

Occasionally, as when lamp cords fray or wear thin, a black hot wire comes in contact with a white neutral wire. When this happens, the current, or circular flow, takes a shortcut. For an instant, the flow increases dramatically. This "hot" surge usually creates a flash that burns away the contact surfaces. With the contact points burned off, the short no longer exists. What is left is a visible black char mark from the spark.

When a short circuit increases current flow beyond the breaker rating, the breaker opens and interrupts the flow. If a short circuit increases flow to a level just below the breaker rating, the breaker will not trip, but some part of the circuit may be destroyed.

Grounding a system

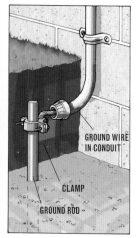

Grounding through copper rods
When possible, the connection should be made below grade.

How your system is grounded will depend upon the age of your home and on specific regulations of your local or municipal code. Many homes are grounded through their water pipes to the city water main. In this case, the grounding wire travels from the panel bus bar to the house side of the water meter. It is then clamped to both sides of the meter. When a ground fault occurs, electricity is drained off through the water service and dissipates in the surrounding soil.

Other homes may be grounded directly through copper grounding rods. In this case, the grounding rod is driven into the ground at least 8 feet deep, usually near an outside basement wall. A simple grounding clamp ties the rod to the ground wire.

Many areas are now requiring that every electrical system be grounded both to the metallic plumbing system and to a ground rod. Other codes require that the grounding electrode travel all the way to the water main on new construction installations. Ask your local code authority for grounding requirements in your area.

A short, or ground fault, often happens when a black (positive) wire comes loose from its terminal and touches a metal outlet box or the metal housing of an electrical tool or appliance. Because a ground wire is attached to the metal surface, the current abandons the white neutral wire and travels back to the panel through the bare ground wire. While much of this misdirected electricity is dissipated in the soil, a great deal of resistance can be generated by the loose contact between the metal and the hot wire. If you touch the metal box or tool, you can become the ground conductor for this high-resistance circuit. This is essentially what happens when people are electrocuted in their workshops or bathrooms.

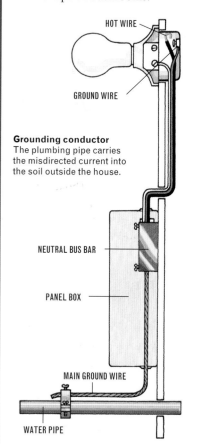

HOT WIRE

GROUND WIRE

Grounding conductor
The plumbing pipe carries the misdirected current into the soil outside the house.

NEUTRAL BUS BAR

PANEL BOX

MAIN GROUND WIRE

WATER PIPE

Grounding individual circuits

Grounding the panel will be of little use if every outlet is not tied to the grounding electrode. The problem is that many older homes have two-wire circuits and two-slot outlets. If your home has three-wire circuits, but two-slot receptacles, you can upgrade to three-slot receptacles.

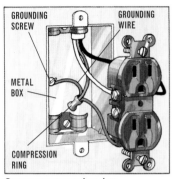

Copper compression ring
All ground wires can be crimped together.

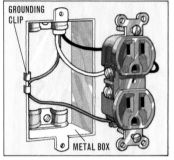

Gounding clip
If no grounding screw is present, use a grounding clip.

Grounded boxes

To determine whether you can make such an upgrade, remove the coverplate and pull the receptacle out of the box, with the power off. If you see a bare wire fastened to the metal box, feel free to install three-slot receptacles. If you see no ground wire in the box, definitely do not convert to three-slot receptacles.

If the box is grounded, you can also use three-prong adapters. Loosen the coverplate screw and slide the grounding wire under the screw. Then tighten the screw and plug the adapter into the receptacle. Every grounded tool or appliance you plug into this adapter will be grounded all the way to soil outside your home.

Ground fault circuit interrupters

As already mentioned, a ground fault can be dangerous. If you touch an appliance or tool that has a loose positive wire, the resistance created there could send a shock through your body. When you are on wet ground or in a damp bathroom, your body improves as a conductor. Water allows you to conduct much more electricity. In damp situations, a ground fault can be fatal.

To protect yourself from a ground fault shock, your bathroom, kitchen, laundry room, and workshop receptacles should be equipped with ground fault circuit interrupters, called GFCIs. GFCIs are now mandatory in bathrooms and garages and in all outdoor wiring. The code also requires GFCIs on outlets near a kitchen sink.

GFCIs work by monitoring the current in the black and white wires. As long as current is equal in both wires, the circuit remains closed. As soon as a GFCI senses an imbalance, as typifies a ground fault, it shuts off the power to that circuit or receptacle within a fraction of a second.

You can acquire GFCI protection with one of three devices. The most expensive and most versatile GFCI is contained in a breaker (1). When you install a GFCI breaker, everything on that circuit is protected. The second device is a GFCI receptacle that is quite easy to install (2). When you install this receptacle, all receptacles on the circuit after the GFCI are also protected. A GFCI receptacle will cost about 30 percent less than a GFCI breaker. The last alternative is the simplest. It is a GFCI receptacle adapter (3). You simply plug this adapter into a standard receptacle and then plug your appliances into the adapter. An adapter works well but protects only the receptacle it is plugged into. Adapters are a good choice in older bathrooms.

To install a GFCI receptacle, turn off power and remove the old receptacle.

Attach all the wires in the box to the new GFCI receptacle.

Screw the new receptacle to the box and add the coverplate.

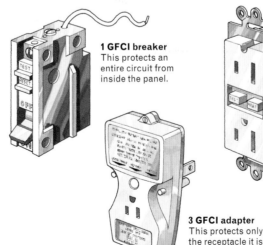

1 GFCI breaker
This protects an entire circuit from inside the panel.

2 GFCI receptacle
This protects the outlet it is in and all outlets after it on a circuit.

3 GFCI adapter
This protects only the receptacle it is plugged into.

Electrical circuits

A s mentioned earlier, a circuit is a flow of electricity that starts at the power source or service panel, continues through the fixtures, and comes back to the source in a continuous pattern. On a practical level, it helps to think of a circuit not as some kind of mysterious flow of electrons but rather as simply a system of wires that carry that flow. It's just easier to visualize wires threaded through our homes, like plumbing pipes carrying water, bringing electricity to our lights and appliances.

Branch circuits

The modern kitchen
A modern kitchen has at least two small-appliance circuits in addition to individual circuits for major appliances. Overhead lights can be part of a general lighting circuit.
1 120-volt, 20-amp circuit for refrigerator/small appliance
2 120-volt, 20-amp circuit for dishwasher
3 120/240-volt circuit to range
4 120-volt, 20-amp circuit for small appliances
5 Dishwasher
6 Range
7 Light switch
8 Overhead lights

The circuits that serve the rooms of your home are called branch circuits. Indeed, if you could see through your home, these wires would look like tree branches, all reaching out from your service panel. In practice, there are three basic kinds of circuits: lighting circuits, small-appliance circuits, and individual circuits.

Lighting circuits serve the general purpose lights and outlets found in living rooms, bedrooms, and bathrooms. They typically power ceiling lights, radios, televisions, lamps, and all manner of low-wattage gadgets.

Small-appliance circuits are commonly found in kitchens and workshops. These circuits have larger wire and higher amp fuses or breakers. They run the usual gamut of small kitchen appliances, such as toasters, food processors, and even refrigerators. The NEC now requires at least two circuits for kitchens, though many older homes get by with only one.

Individual circuits are dedicated to only one appliance. These include 240-volt circuits that serve clothes dryers and water heaters but can include refrigerators, air conditioners, microwave ovens, computers, and dishwashers. As a good rule of thumb, any appliance rated at 1000 watts or greater should have its own circuit and breaker. Many individual circuits carry 240 volts to meet the greater demands of the appliances involved. Others, like computer and microwave oven circuits, might be dedicated for other reasons. Computers are very sensitive to voltage dips and spikes and so are sometimes given a circuit of their own and a switch with an isolated ground terminal. Microwave ovens, on the other hand, create voltage irregularities and so are better kept on their own current.

While your service panel may be rated at 100 amps, you can't commit that many amps to it. When a system is loaded to maximum capacity, conductors and connectors heat up and expand. When demand decreases, conductors and connectors cool and contract. This continual movement eventually loosens connections, creating a fire hazard.

For this reason, the NEC requires that you leave 20 percent of your panel's capacity in reserve. The method for calculating that reserve is called derating. Your system will be different, but the following example will show you how to use the derating method to figure your expansion capabilities.

Assume a 1000-square-foot home with a 100-amp service panel, two small-appliance circuits, a laundry circuit, and two heavy-duty circuits for a range and a clothes dryer. (Heavy-duty circuits are not derated. Also, the formula used to calculate heating and air-conditioning demands is complicated, so those factors have been left out of this example.)

Start by assigning 3 watts to each square foot of living space (3000 watts), 1500 watts to each small appliance circuit, and 1500 watts to the laundry circuit. This yields a subtotal of 7500 watts for all 120-volt circuits. Of this 7500 watts, figure the first 3000 watts at 100 percent and the remaining 4500 watts at 35 percent. Add the derated figure (1575 watts) to the original 3000 watts for a subtotal of 4575 watts. Finally, assign full-load ratings to the two heavy-duty circuits (8000 and 5500 watts). Add these to the derated subtotal for a derated total of 18,075 watts. Because watts equal volts times amps, divide 18,075 watts by 240 volts, for a total of 75.3125, or 75 amps. Since a 100-amp service can be loaded to only 80 amps in the derated system, your expansion potential is limited to 5 amps.

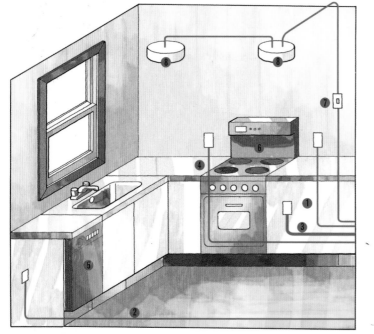

The number of circuits your home should have depends mostly on its size and on your own special needs. The NEC requires one circuit for every 600 square feet of floor space, but many electricians prefer a 1/500 ratio to cover future needs. In the final analysis, your lifestyle, personal needs, and your plans for the future have the most to do with how many circuits you install. For example, if you are converting a den into an entertainment center, your electrical needs in that room will be greater than before. If you plan to expand into the attic, you should keep that in mind when you plan your circuits.

Adding outlets to a circuit

If you don't need a new circuit but would appreciate a few more outlets, you may be able to add outlets to existing circuits. If you determine that a 15-amp circuit has less than 10 outlets or a 20-amp circuit has less than 13, you can cut new boxes where you need them and run wire from one of the existing boxes to the first new box. From there on, you simply run wire from one box to another in sequence and install new receptacles.

Making room in a full panel

In many cases, expansion will seem impossible because no fuse or breaker slots are left in the panel. If this is the case in your home, don't panic. Expansion may still be possible by attaching a new subpanel or by combining circuits in the existing service panel.

The easiest and sometimes only route is to combine circuits. The first step is to determine which two circuits serve so few outlets that together they could be protected by a single fuse or breaker. For example, each outlet is given a rating of 1.5 amps, so a 15-amp breaker can protect 10 outlets. If you find one circuit that serves four outlets and another circuit that serves six, those two circuits can be combined. Kitchen circuits can't be combined.

To combine circuits, remove each wire from its breaker slot or fuse terminal and tie both wires and a short pigtail (a 4- to 6-inch piece of wire) together with a wire connector. Then tie the pigtail wire to the fuse terminal or breaker. This will leave one circuit vacant for expansion.

To combine circuits, remove black wire from one breaker.

Join black wires to pigtail wire with wire connector.

Remove black wire from breaker for second circuit.

Attach pigtail to one breaker and circuits are combined.

Until recently, when 60-amp service panels were filled to capacity with fuses and wires, you could tie onto the tap screws between the four fuses and create a new subpanel. The NEC has disallowed this practice because the tap screws, sometimes called water-heater taps, are not properly fused. The new ruling allows only six 120-volt circuits or one 240-volt circuit and four 120-volt circuits in a 60-amp panel.

If you do have room in the panel, a subpanel is still a good way to run several circuits to a remote location. If you need to run to an attic or an outbuilding, you can run one heavier wire to a subpanel and then let the subpanel serve several remote circuits.

Start by running the cable between panel locations. Then attach the wires to the subpanel first. Your subpanel may have fuses or breakers. If yours has fuses, attach the hot wires to the fuse terminals. If your subpanel has breakers, attach the hot wires to the main disconnect breaker.

The white neutral wire should attach to a neutral bus in the subpanel. Some subpanel boxes have only one bus bar for attaching the neutral and ground wires. These panels have to be grounded with a separate grounding cable attached to a grounding rod outside the house. Subpanels with separate neutral and grounding buses don't need the dedicated grounding wire. They are grounded through the cable that goes back to the main service panel and into the main grounding rod.

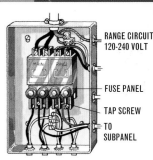
RANGE CIRCUIT 120-240 VOLT
FUSE PANEL
TAP SCREW
TO SUBPANEL
This method is no longer allowed

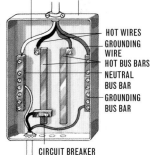
HOT WIRES   MAIN DISCONNECT
NEUTRAL BUS
HOT BUS BARS
BREAKER
TO SUBPANEL
NEUTRAL GROUND
GROUNDING ELECTRODE
Subpanel with single neutral bus

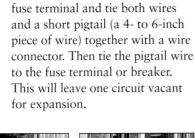
NEUTRAL WIRE   SUBPANEL
HOT WIRES
GROUNDING WIRE
HOT BUS BARS
NEUTRAL BUS BAR
GROUNDING BUS BAR
CIRCUIT BREAKER
Subpanel with neutral and ground buses

Extending circuits

Drilling
When drilling holes through studs and joists, drill only within the middle third of the board. Never, under any circumstances, notch the bottom of a joist. A notch on the bottom side of a joist seriously threatens its load-carrying capacity. And when you drill near the edge of a stud, you are running the cable within reach of drywall fasteners. If you must drill near the edge of a stud or joist (less than 1¼ inches) cover that section of the framing member with a ⅟₁₆-inch -thick protection plate.

A typical knob-and-tube extension
1 New circuit
2 Existing knob-and-tube wiring
3 Cable clamp
4 Grounding wire to neutral bus or to cold-water pipe
5 Soldered splice
6 Loom clamp
7 Junction box
8 Tube
9 Knob

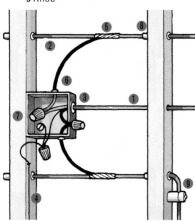

There are several possible methods for extending circuits. The approach that will be best for you depends on available space in the service panel and your existing wiring. Several options are discussed below.

Extending a knob-and-tube circuit

If you own one of the many thousands of homes with old knob-and-tube wiring, expansion is difficult but not impossible. Knob-and-tube is a two-wire system with each individual wire encased in treated fabric. The wires run side by side through ceramic insulators, called knobs, that are nailed to joists or rafters, and through ceramic tubes that are inserted in holes drilled in studs.

Knob-and-tube wiring can no longer be installed under current codes, but it can be extended, providing you follow a fairly strict procedure. Start by shutting the power off to the circuit to be extended. Then install a square junction box between or near the two knob-and-tube wires.

Next, run 14/2 with ground cable from the new outlets to this junction box and clamp the cable in the box. Strip the sheathing from the cable so that you have three 6-inch leads (one black, one white, one ground) in the box. Then strip about 2 inches of insulation from both knob-and-tube wires near the junction box. Cut one black and one white TW wire long enough to reach the knob-and-tube wires. Slide these wires into a sheath made for this type of work

called a loom. Then clamp the loom-covered TW wires to the box with approved clamps.

To tie the TW wires to the knob-and-tube wires, first wrap each TW wire tightly around its knob-and-tube wire so that the wrap is at least ¾-inch long within the stripped area of the old wire. Then solder the connections with rosin-core solder. Hold a soldering iron to the wires until the solder melts and adheres to the wires. When the solder has cooled, wrap the exposed portions of the wire with electrical tape. For added protection, continue the tape at least 2 inches past the joint on each side.

With the soldered connections made, move back down to the junction box and join the cable leads to the TW wires with wire connectors. To ground the extension circuit, first mount a grounding pigtail to the back of the box. Then run a separate ground wire to the service panel or the nearest cold-water plumbing pipe. Screw this wire to the neutral bus bar in the panel or clamp it to the plumbing pipe with a proper fitting. Then return to the box and join the cable ground wire, the separate ground wire, and the pigtail with a wire connector.

Using skinny breakers

If your service panel is a newer breaker model, but all the breaker slots are filled, you may be able to get one more circuit by substituting two extra narrow breakers. Euphemistically called "skinnies," these

narrow breakers allow you to attach one breaker to the existing circuit and another to a new circuit. Both breakers are then inserted in the space formerly occupied by the standard-size breaker.

Common circuit routes

How you get from here to there with a circuit is largely a matter of choice. However, it can be greatly influenced by the layout of the house and by whether you are wiring a new house or expanding the wiring in an older one. Circuits in new homes generally take a direct route, while new circuits in existing homes find the path of least resistance, both physically and financially.

As you plan your circuits, think

first about how you will get from the service panel to the outlet area. Plan for the most economical use of cable. The cost of cable or conduit and wires makes long circuits more costly, of course, and long circuits also offer more resistance to the flow of current and, therefore, greater chance for overheating.

When possible, run several cables through the same holes until each must branch off to its own service area. This will result in fewer holes in load-bearing joists and less time spent drilling them. Usually you'll have a lot of holes to drill so it makes sense to reduce that number when you can.

Outlet and fixture boxes

Outlet and fixture boxes now are made of metal, nonmetallic composition material, or plastic. Plastic boxes cost substantially less than the others and in most situations work just as well. There is, however, a notable practical difference. When wiring into metal boxes, you must attach the ground wires to the box. Plastic and nonmetallic materials are poor conductors, and therefore can't be used for grounding a circuit. In plastic or nonmetallic boxes, you tie all middle-of-run ground wires together and attach the end-of-run ground wire to the receptacle grounding terminal. Aside from this basic difference, wire is clamped to metal and nonmetallic boxes, whereas in plastic boxes, wire is held in place by staples driven into framing members or with self-gripping plastic tabs.

MAXIMUM NUMBER OF WIRES PER BOX

Size of box	No.14	No.12	No.10
Round or octagonal			
4 X 1½"	7	6	6
4 X 2⅛"	10	9	8
Square			
4 X 1½"	10	9	8
4 X 2⅛"	15	13	12
Switch Boxes			
3 X 2 X 2¼"	5	4	4
3 X 2 X 2½"	6	5	5
3 X 2 X 2¾"	7	6	5
3 X 2 X 3½"	9	8	7
Junction Boxes			
4 X 2⅛ X 1⅞"	6	5	5
4 X 2⅛ X 2⅛"	7	6	5

All ground wires in a box can be counted as one wire.

Metal box cover
If you have a lot of different boxes to install, one way to simplify the job is to install the same metal double box for each location. Then just add a metal cover designed for the specific box use: double or single switch or receptacle or ceiling fixture.

Which box should you use

The shape of a box is your best clue to its intended use. Round boxes are most frequently used with ceiling fixtures, while square or rectangular boxes most often contain switches or receptacles mounted in the walls. While wall fixtures and special adapter plates allow some crossover, shape is still a good indicator.

New-work boxes are designed to be attached directly to studs or rafters. A variety of fastening devices, including screws, nails, brackets, and bars hold these boxes in place. Cut-in (sometimes called old-work) boxes, on the other hand, attach directly to the surface materials between studs or joists. Take the time to familiarize yourself with the many kinds of boxes and their varied applications. When the time comes to start a project, you will know just which boxes to buy.

Wall and ceiling boxes

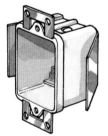
Plastic cut-in wall box

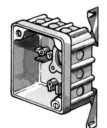
Nonmetallic wall box

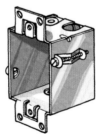
Metal wall box

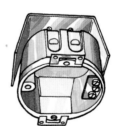
Plastic cut-in ceiling box

Metal ceiling box

Methods of mounting

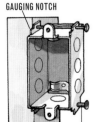
GAUGING NOTCH
DRIVE NAILS
Nail-in box

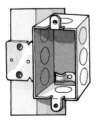
L-bracket wall box

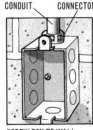
CONDUIT   CONNECTOR
SCREW BOX TO WALL WITH ANCHORS
Utility (handy) box

JOIST
Hanger bracket box

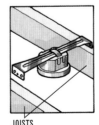
JOISTS
Bar hanger box

L-bracket ceiling box

Switches

Switches for special needs

Switches are used to open and close circuits. When in the closed position, the circuit is completed and current flows according to demand. When in the open position, the circuit is interrupted and current cannot complete the circuit.

Basic switches

There are four basic types of switches. The one most frequently used is the single-pole switch. Single-pole switches are used to open or close simple two-wire circuits. The next most frequently used is a three-way switch. Three-way switches are most often used to provide two switching locations for a single overhead light. The third most common is the four-way switch, which allows you to control an appliance from three or more locations. The fourth type is the double-pole switch. This device can handle two hot wires and is therefore commonly used to switch 240-volt outlets and appliances. Like single-pole switches, double-poles have "on" and "off" toggle positions.

In addition to the four basic types, switches are also made for special needs and with special features. Some of these switches are just slightly more convenient than the basic models. But others offer real advantages, like dimmer switches, locking switches, lighted toggle switches, and others shown below. Consider installing one of these special switches to make a part of your life a little easier. Almost all are simple to install; it's usually just a matter of pulling out your current switch and replacing it with the new one, using the same box and wire.

Dimmer switches
Dimmer switches, or rheostats, are popular because they allow you to adjust standard lighting fixtures to create different lighting effects. Low light makes a room seem warmer and more inviting, while brighter light offers a better work environment. Dimmer switches give you both options and everything in between. If used properly, dimmer switches can also save energy by using less wattage.

Locking switches
Locking switches do not have "on/off" toggles, but require a key to operate. These switches are ideal for protecting electrical tools, computers, or stereo equipment from children. Simply switch an entire tool circuit off with a locking switch.

Lighted toggle switches
These switches are ideal for basement or garage use. The toggle lever contains a tiny light that remains on when the light is shut off. The light uses very little energy and will save you from having to feel your way to the switch in the dark.

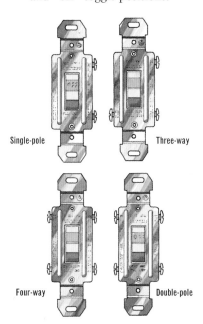

Single-pole

Three-way

Four-way

Double-pole

Toggle switches

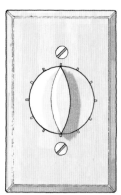

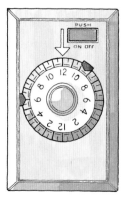

Time-delay switches
Time-delay switches are perfect for those situations where you need to get from here to there before the light goes out. The most frequent use of a time-delay switch is on a flood light between a garage and house. You can turn the time-delay switch off in the garage and still have time to unlock the back door before the light goes out.

Time-clock switches
Time-clock switches can be set to come on or go off at programmed intervals. They are commonly used to discourage burglars. They allow you to simulate your regular lighting habits when away.

Pilot-light switches
Pilot-light switches tell you when they are on. If you have trouble remembering to shut the backyard light off, the glowing light will help you remember.

Replacing a switch

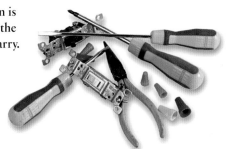

If you have never looked closely at a switch, now is a good time. A great deal of information is stamped into the metal yoke and the plastic body of a switch. You will see the amp rating, the volt rating, the approved wire type, the testing lab's approval, and the type of current it can carry. Newer models will also give you a gauge to show you how much wire to strip from the conductors. And if you make a mistake pushing the wires into the push-in terminals, the release slots are even marked so you can pull the wires back out without damaging the switch. Probably the most important designations on a switch are the UL approval stamp and the CO/ALR rating. The UL listing is your assurance of quality and the CO/ALR rating tells you that that particular switch can be safely used with aluminum, aluminum-clad, or copper wires.

Replacing a single-pole switch

Switches do eventually wear out. They may quit with one flick of the toggle, or they may work once in a while if you push on the toggle just right. In either case, there is no need to put up with a faulty switch. Single-pole switches are not expensive and are easy to replace.

Start by shutting the power off to the circuit serving the bad switch. Then remove the cover-plate and loosen the screws on the mounting yoke. Pull the switch out of the box so that you can work on it. You will notice that both wires fastened to the switch terminals are black. Because a switch needs only to control the hot side of the circuit, this makes perfect sense. You will also notice that the white wires are simply tied together and are not involved with the switch at all.

Check to make sure that your replacement looks like the faulty switch. It may have newer push-in terminals in addition to the screw terminals, but it should have only two. Because the existing conductors will be shaped to fit the screw terminals, skip the push-in option and just use the terminals. Remove the old switch and attach the black wires to the new switch terminals. It will not matter which black wire you connect to which terminal. Slip the hook-shaped wires under the new screws so the open side of the hook is facing right, or clockwise. Then tighten the screws.

Usually there's no grounding screw on a switch. To maintain proper circuit grounding, just join the cable ground wires and a

pigtail wire together with a wire connector or compression ring. Attach the other end of the pigtail to the grounding screw at the back of the box. If your switch has a grounding screw, run a pigtail from this screw to the other cable ground wires and to a pigtail that goes to the grounding screw at the back of the box. Push the switch into the box, attach the yoke to the box, and replace the coverplate.

Typical pigtail connection
A "pigtail" is a short piece of wire used as a lead to a receptacle, switch, or fixture. A typical pigtail wire is about 6 inches long and is stripped on both ends. One end attaches to a terminal and the other is joined to the circuit wires in a wire connector. Because pigtails are so often used for joining ground wires to the grounding screw in a metal box, pigtails with a grounding screw attached are commonly available.

Typical single-pole switch connection

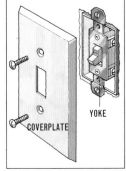

Coverplate screws mount to yoke

Aluminum wires and switches
To avoid the the hazards of aluminum wiring (page 17), use CO/ALR-rated switches when connecting aluminum wire directly to switches. CU/AL switches can be used with aluminum wire if an indirect connection is made. In this case, a copper pigtail attaches to the switch and is then joined to the aluminum wire in a wire connector filled with antioxidation compound. Never use aluminum wires in push-in terminals.

Connecting to terminals

Many switches come with push-in terminals and binding screw terminals. You can use either one, but the push-in terminals are easier. The gauge on the back of a push-in switch shows you exactly how much insulation to strip from each conductor. If you strip too

much or too little insulation, you should redo the connection. To release the locking clip inside the switch, insert a piece of wire into the release slot next to the terminal and press in. At the same time, push the conductor in slightly and then pull it out.

Push-in terminal connection **Screw-type terminal connection**

35

Three-way and four-way switches

Three- and four-way switches allow you to control a single overhead light from two or three locations. This is especially handy when that light is at the top of stairs or in the middle of a large room. Instead of making your way across a darkened room or up dark stairs, you can shut the light off when you leave the area, no matter which end you are on.

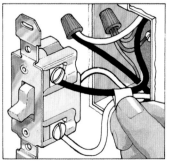

Installing three- and four-way switches
This can be a complicated and time-consuming procedure. You have to cut in new boxes and run new cable through finished walls, ceilings, or floors. For instructions on installing new wiring in existing houses, see pages 45 to 50.

TRAVELER TERMINAL   MASKING TAPE

A typical three-way hookup
Tape the common hot wire

Replacing a four-way switch

Four-way switches allow control of a single fixture from three locations. Four-ways have four terminals and are used in conjunction with 2 three-way switches. If a continuity test shows a bad four-way switch, replace it.

A four-way switch receives two traveler wires, one from each three-way cable attached to the 2 three-way switches. To replace a four-way switch, shut off the power and pull the switch from the box. Then disconnect the top two travelers and connect them to the top two terminals of the new switch. Do the same with the bottom two travelers. By transferring only two wires at a time, you will avoid making a wiring mistake.

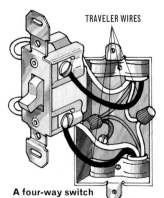

TRAVELER WIRES

A three-way circuit loop
1 Light fixture
2 Two-wire w/ground cable
3 First switch
4 Three-wire w/ground cable
5 Second switch

A four-way switch

Replacing a three-way switch

If you have one three-way switch, you must have another. If one of them fails, you will have to check both (with a continuity tester) in order to isolate the defective switch. When you've determined which switch no longer works, shut off the power to that circuit. Then remove the coverplate and mounting yoke screws and pull the switch out of the box. To protect yourself further, test the circuit conductors with a voltage tester.

With 2 three-way switches, three options are required: on/off, off/on, and off/off. When you pull a three-way switch out of its box, you will see that it has three terminals and a grounding screw. Like single-pole switches, three-ways control only hot wires. You may see a red wire, a black wire, and a white wire attached to the three terminals, but all are considered hot. Two of these hot wires are "travelers" and one is a common wire. The common wire will be attached to the third terminal, which will be marked either "COM" or will have a darker colored screw. The two travelers will be attached to matching screws of a lighter color.

When replacing a defective three-way switch, start by marking the common wire with a piece of tape. Then remove each wire from its terminal. Attach the two travelers to the two like-colored terminals of the new switch. It doesn't matter which terminal gets which traveler. Then fasten the common wire to the darker, or marked, screw. If the ground wire was connected to the defective switch only, use a pigtail to attach it to the new switch and to the metal box. If the box is plastic, attach a pigtail from the switch to the other ground wires.

Creating a three-way circuit loop

If one of your ceiling lights is still an old-fashioned pull-chain model, you may want to install a new fixture that can be controlled from either side of the room.

Start by shutting off the power to the circuit. Undo the old ceiling fixture so that you have access to the wiring in the box. Then check to see how best to run the new switch loop. When you have determined which is the easiest route to the new switch locations, install cut-in boxes at the appropriate locations. Then fish a 14/2 with ground cable from the ceiling box, across the ceiling, and down one wall to the first switch box.

From the first box, run a 14/3 with ground cable to the second switch box. Fasten the new cables to the new boxes and to the ceiling box. Allow about eight inches of cable to extend past the opening of each box to make working easier.

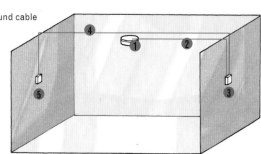

Strip seven inches of sheathing off each cable, and ⅜ inch of insulation off each wire. Then connect the new fixture leads to the ceiling cable with wire connectors and attach the switch wires to the switches. Ground all boxes properly and restore power to the circuit.

Special-use switches

Special-use switches can make your lighting more effective and useful. Lighted switches are easier to see; dimmer switches can create softer moods and save money, too. The special switches shown on page 34 are not expensive and are easy to install. Each should come with wiring diagrams to suit a variety of situations.

Installing dimmer switches

To install a simple three-position dimmer switch on a two-wire circuit, shut off the power to the circuit and remove the single-pole switch. Shutting off the power here is doubly important because of the electronic circuits in the switch. A spark could easily ruin its diode rectifier. Then connect the black wire to the positive terminal and the white wire to the

neutral terminal, just as you would a single-pole switch. Attach the ground to the box or switch; replace the switch and coverplate. These three-position switches can carry a maximum of 300 watts, so don't use them on circuits that require more wattage.

For circuits that serve up to 600 watts, use a dimmer switch with a knob-controlled rheostat. These

too are wired just like a standard single-pole switch, unless you need a three-way version or a special fluorescent dimmer.

Three-way dimmer switches are wired the same as standard three-way switches but will often come with wire leads instead of terminals. In this case, you will make all connections inside the box with wire connectors.

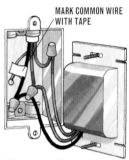

MARK COMMON WIRE WITH TAPE

Three-way dimmer switch

Installing a pilot-light switch

Pilot-light switches come in two varieties, but both must be installed in middle-of-the-run boxes. One has the light inside the toggle switch and the other has a larger light below a horizontal toggle. The lighted toggle version takes a switch coverplate and the separate light version requires a receptacle coverplate. They are wired a little differently, but perform the same task. Before starting any switch replacement, be sure to shut the power off to that circuit.

If you choose the toggle-light version, you will find two brass terminals at the top of the switch and one silver-colored terminal at the bottom of the switch. Remove the single-pole switch and attach

the incoming and outgoing black wires to the brass terminals on the new switch. Then join the incoming and outgoing white neutral wires to a pigtail inside the box and run the other end of the pigtail to the silver terminal on the new switch. Finish by attaching the ground wires to the metal box or to the ground screw on the switch. If after restoring power to the circuit, the pilot light stays on in the off position, reverse the black wires on the switch.

If you choose the separate light version, you will find three brass terminals and a silver terminal. Attach the outgoing black wire to the side with two brass terminals; either terminal will do. Then

connect the incoming black wire to the brass screw on the other side of the switch. Finally, tie the white neutral to the silver screw terminal with a pigtail and connect the ground to the back of the metal box.

Push the switch back into the box, taking care not to push any wires away from the terminal screws. Then fasten the yoke screws to the box and install the coverplate. Test your work. The light should come on when the switch is turned on.

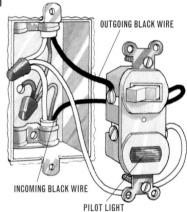

OUTGOING BLACK WIRE

INCOMING BLACK WIRE

PILOT LIGHT

Installing time-clock switches

Like pilot-light switches, time-clock switches can be installed only in middle-of-the-run outlets. You will also need to use a voltage tester to locate the incoming black conductor. Time-clock switches sometimes come with wire leads instead of terminals.

Start by shutting the power off and removing the old switch. Then fasten the special mounting bracket to the box. Tie the black lead to the incoming black wire and the red wire to the outgoing black wire. Connect the white neutral wire to the circuit neutral wires and the

ground wire to the box. Screw the switch to the mounting bracket and restore power.

A time-clock switch

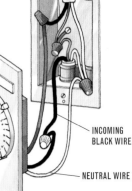

OUTGOING BLACK WIRE

INCOMING BLACK WIRE

NEUTRAL WIRE

Receptacles

There are several reasons why you might want to replace a receptacle. You may need to upgrade from two-socket to three-socket outlets to match your three-prong plugs. Of course, the circuit must be grounded if you intend to make this upgrade. But in most cases, you install a new receptacle because the old one no longer works. If a fuse blows or a breaker trips only when you plug an appliance into a given receptacle, that receptacle is probably faulty. When receptacles fail, they often cause a short circuit, which in turn trips a breaker.

In general, there are two basic types of receptacles you can buy. One is side-wired and features binding screw terminals on both sides. The other is back-wired and features the newer push-in terminals. If you are working with older wire that has already been shaped to fit under terminal screws, it's usually easier to use side-wired replacement receptacles. If you are working with new wire or don't mind cutting and stripping existing wire, then go ahead and use back-wired receptacles.

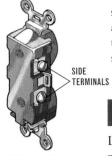

SIDE
TERMINALS

**Side-wired
receptacle**

RELEASE
SLOT

PUSH-IN
TERMINALS

**Back-wired,
push-in terminals**

Reading receptacles

Like switches, receptacles are marked with a variety of symbols that you should check before you buy. The amp and voltage ratings will be stamped on the body, as will the testing lab's name and approval symbol. The mounting yoke may also tell you what type of wire each receptacle is approved to carry. If you are connecting solid copper wire, a CU CLAD rating is sufficient. If you are connecting aluminum wire, a CO/ALR rating is a must. If you connect aluminum wiring

directly to an unapproved receptacle, you are risking a fire or at the very least the regular annoyance of tripped breakers or blown fuses.

The NEC does allow CU CLAD receptacles to be used with aluminum wire if the receptacle connection is made with a copper pigtail. However, the wire connector joining the aluminum wire and the copper pigtail must be filled with antioxidation compound to keep air from stimulating corrosion.

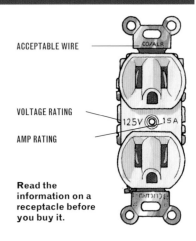

ACCEPTABLE WIRE

VOLTAGE RATING

AMP RATING

**Read the
information on a
receptacle before
you buy it.**

Receptacle switches

**Switch/receptacle
combination**

A receptacle/switch combination offers greater versatility in a single box. These models are popular in simple remodeling projects where additional boxes are not feasible or practical.

This combination can be wired together or separately. For example, the switch might control a bathroom exhaust fan and light, while the receptacle half could be wired directly, so that it is always hot. In another situation, where

an appliance needs to be controlled by a switch, the switch half of the combination would control the receptacle half. This combination is one way to add a receptacle to an older bathroom without a major rewiring project. Of course, every bathroom and appliance circuit must be protected by a ground fault interrupter to meet code. In this case, the GFCI would probably be installed in the panel. GFCI

receptacles are also available for ungrounded circuits. Check with your local electrical supply outlet for your best alternative.

Receptacle/switch devices cannot be installed in end-of-the-run boxes. Because every receptacle requires both a positive and a neutral terminal, and switches control only the positive sides of circuits, only middle-of-the-run configurations will do.

Plastic wire connectors (trade name Wire Nuts) are used for joining wires in fixtures, appliances, circuit boxes, and service panels. Any joint made with a wire connector must remain accessible, so they can't be used on cable that is hidden behind a wall or ceiling. Plastic wire connectors are easy to use (you just twist them onto the ends of the wires being joined), inexpensive, and available in any hardware store or home center. Be sure to pick the one that's designed for the wires you are splicing.

Gray connector
The smallest commonly available wire connector, it can hold a minimum of one No. 20 with one No. 22 wire, and a maximum of two No. 16 wires.

Blue connector
It can hold a minimum of three No. 22 wires and a maximum of three No. 16 wires.

Orange connector
It can hold a minimum of three No. 22 and a maximum of two No. 14 with one No. 18.

Yellow connector
This can hold a minimum of one No. 14 with one No. 18 and a maximum of one No. 10 with one No. 14.

Red connector
This can hold a minimum of two No. 14 and a maximum of four No. 12.

Pigtail connections
Some municipal codes require that all standard receptacle connections be made with pigtail leads. In this case, the black pigtail is tied to one brass terminal and the white pigtail is tied to a silver terminal on the opposite side of the receptacle. In this way, one faulty terminal connection cannot disable an entire circuit. While this practice is not part of the NEC, local authorities may enforce its use. In any case, a pigtail should be used whenever more than one wire must be tied to a single terminal.

There are two basic wiring methods for standard receptacles. The method you use will depend upon where the receptacle is located in the circuit. If the receptacle you are about to install is in the middle of the circuit, you will follow the middle-of-the-run wiring method. If it is the last receptacle on a circuit, you will follow the end-of-run method.

Installing middle-of-the-run receptacles

Because a middle-of-the-run receptacle must pass electricity along to other receptacles on a circuit, it must be wired accordingly. A middle-of-the-run outlet box will contain two cables carrying six wires: two black, two white, and two bare ground wires.

To wire a middle-of-the-run receptacle, tie the two black wires to the two brass-colored terminals. Then attach the two white wires to the two silver-colored terminals. To ground a receptacle in a metal box, make a pigtail connection between the two bare ground wires and the ground screw on the receptacle. Then attach another pigtail to the box with a machine screw or bonding clip. If installing a receptacle in a nonmetallic box, simply tie the ground wires to the receptacle ground.

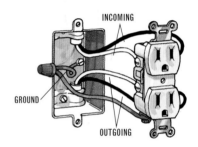

Installing end-of-the-run receptacles

An end-of-the-run receptacle only needs to be wired so that the circuit is completed across its own terminals. To wire an end-of-the-run receptacle, simply tie the single black wire to the brass terminal and the single white wire to the silver terminal. Then pigtail from the incoming ground wire to the ground screw on the receptacle and to the metal box. If working with a nonmetallic box, tie the ground wire directly to the receptacle ground screw.

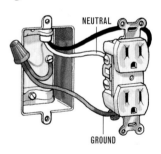

Armored cable and receptacles

Some older homes have armored cable, or BX, instead of sheathed cable. Some armored cable uses the metal armor as a grounding conductor and has no separate ground wire. To ground a receptacle with armored cable that doesn't have a ground wire, use a pigtail between the box and the receptacle ground screw. Because the metal box is fastened to the metal cable, a permanent ground connection is made.

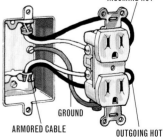

Installing switch/receptacle combinations

If you have a switch where you also need a receptacle, you can often have both in one unit. A switch/receptacle combination gives you both, while allowing you to use the wiring already in the switch box. But before buying a switch/receptacle unit, make sure you know which wiring method you will be able to use. The location of the unit on a circuit will dictate how the switch/receptacle will work.

The most popular use of a switch/receptacle combination has the receptacle wired hot and the switch controlling a remote light or small appliance. Because the receptacle must have both a hot and a neutral wire to complete the circuit, this switch/receptacle combination must be installed in a middle-of-the-run location. If you want the switch to control the outlet and the light, you will have to pull another cable to get a neutral for the receptacle.

To wire a switch/receptacle to a middle-of-the-run outlet, join the white neutral wires with a wire connector and pigtail to the silver-colored terminal screw. Attach the incoming black wire to one of the brass screws and the black outgoing switch wire to the copper screw. Then ground the receptacle and box with a pigtail to the receptacle ground screw.

To have the switch control the receptacle and the light at the same time, reverse the black wires. The incoming black wire should be connected to the copper screw and the outgoing black switch wire should be connected to the brass-colored screw.

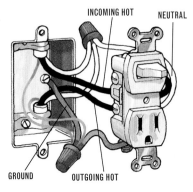

The switch controls a remote light

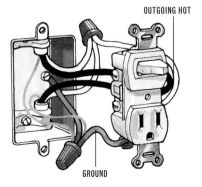

The switch controls the receptacle

Installing a receptacle/light combination

Like a receptacle /switch combination, a receptacle/light combination is a good way to gain a receptacle without the work and expense of installing new boxes. Receptacle/light combination units are most commonly used over bathroom lavatories, but can be installed elsewhere. They are usually rated at 15 amps, so only low-wattage appliances should be plugged into them. Electric razors and hair dryers will not overload receptacle/light combinations. Because the NEC requires every bathroom outlet to be protected from ground fault, a receptacle light should always be protected by a GFCI.

Receptacle/light combinations can be wired in two ways. A switch can control both the light and the receptacle, or the receptacle half of the fixture can be wired hot, leaving the switch to control only the light (see "Switching half of a receptacle" on facing page). How you wire your own depends on whether your existing light is in an end-of-the-run or middle-of-the-run outlet box.

If only two wires enter your existing fixture box, you are dealing with an end-of-the-run connection, in which case both the receptacle and the light must be operated by the switch.

If you find four wires (plus a ground) in your existing box, you will be able to wire the receptacle hot and switch the light independently.

Switching half of a receptacle

If most of the lights you use in your living room and bedrooms are lamps instead of permanent light fixtures, you may wish to wire half of some receptacles to switches. In this case, the bottom half of each outlet is wired directly and is always hot. TVs and other small appliances can be plugged into those. All lamps, on the other hand, could then be plugged into the switch half of the receptacles. The obvious advantage of this arrangement is that you can turn on lamps as you come through the door.

To split a receptacle so that half of it is hot full time and the other half is switch-controlled, start with the receptacle. As you hold a receptacle with the sockets facing you, you will see that the terminals on both sides are tied together with metal strips. You will also see that the strips have metal tabs that are scored part way through. These metal strips join both halves of the receptacle, which is what allows you to wire to only one terminal on each side and still have power to both sockets.

In the case of a split receptacle, you will no longer want the top and bottom sockets tied together on the hot side. To separate the top and bottom sockets, use pliers and break the tab off the metal strip on the hot side only. Do not break the tab on the neutral side.

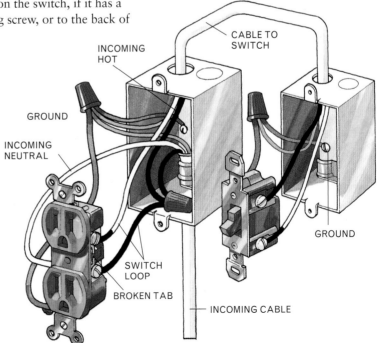

Split receptacles
To separate the top half of a receptacle from the bottom half, break the connecting tab.

Wiring split receptacles

To wire a split receptacle to a switch, use 14/2 with ground cable. Bring this three-wire cable from the power source to the receptacle box and then continue it to the switch box.

Fishing this cable through finished walls and ceilings can be difficult and time consuming. If you have access to the room from a basement directly below or an attic directly above, the job is easier. From the basement you just drill up through the bottom wall plates to the stud spaces that hold the receptacle boxes. From the attic, drill through the wall top plates into the stud spaces. Take accurate measurements in the room to be sure that you drill in the right places.

At the receptacle box, connect the outgoing white wire to a brass terminal. In this case, the white wire will be the hot wire of the switch loop. To keep it straight, code it with a piece of black tape.

Then tie all the black wires together and pigtail over to the remaining brass terminal. This will leave only the ground wires unattached in the receptacle box. Tie them together with a double pigtail. Tie one pigtail to the box and the other to the ground terminal on the receptacle.

To connect the switch, all you will have to do is tie the black wire to one terminal and the white to the other. Then tie the ground wire to the ground terminal on the switch, if it has a grounding screw, or to the back of the box.

CABLE TO SWITCH

INCOMING HOT

GROUND

INCOMING NEUTRAL

SWITCH LOOP

BROKEN TAB

GROUND

INCOMING CABLE

New wiring for new rooms

If you will be wiring a new home, new addition, or gutted older home, getting wiring from here to there seems an easy task. It is, in fact, much easier than fighting the structural barriers in remodeling work. Even so, there are plenty of practical decisions to make, including the most efficient use of costly materials.

Start with a well-considered plan on paper. Work it out so you know where your receptacles, lights, and switches will be. Decide in advance how many circuits you will need. And don't forget future needs while you are at it.

How many outlets

Installing a recessed light fixture in the ceiling.

Cut hole, feed switch cable to light box, and join wires.

Angle mounting bracket on light into hole and attach to joists.

Slide trim ring onto light, snap in place, and install bulb.

The number of receptacles, switches, and fixtures you install should be determined by need. Just remember, it's far easier to install extra boxes now than it will be later.

The NEC has its own minimum standard that must be followed: at least one receptacle for every 12 feet of wall space. Any short wall 2 feet long or longer must have one. And you must put one within 6 feet of every entry door.

Even with these rules, the layout of a home may be confusing. If, for example, you measure 12 feet from one box to another, and the 12-foot location happens to fall in the middle of a closet-door space, what then? You would have to place the receptacle before the door, even if this means only 9 feet between the two boxes. The next box in line must be 12 feet from the last one even though it was just 9 feet from the one before. It may seem like a lot of receptacles, but after you start using them, you'll probably wish you had more.

Planning light locations

NEC lighting regulations are few, and, in general, involve safety, not practicality. The two areas of concern are fire protection and injury prevention.

Closet lighting
Lights in closets are not mandatory. Many builders prefer to let a ceiling fixture from an adjacent room spill light into a closet. In so doing, they avoid having to comply with some fairly stringent NEC codes concerning closet lighting.

The chief concern of code authorities and fire officials is that stored blankets and clothing would come in contact with exposed lights, thereby creating a fire hazard. In fact, many fires do start in closets every year. To guard against this possibility, exposed lights are prohibited in any closet less than 40 inches deep. In closets deeper than 40 inches, exposed lights must be at least 18 inches from combustible materials. The space between the bulb and the floor must also be unobstructed.

If your closets cannot be fitted with surface-mounted fixtures, you can circumvent the space requirements by installing recessed lights. Recessed lights have their own limitations, however. Those installed in closets must meet certain heat-resistance specifications and must also have solid lens covers. Recessed lights with solid lens covers and the correct heat rating can be used with a 6-inch clearance to combustibles.

Recessed lighting
Recessed light fixtures should be approved by your local code authority and fire department. Recessed lights are hidden in inverted canisters. These canisters can become quite hot and have

caused quite a few fires in the past. Most started when homeowners blew cellulose insulation into their attics without protecting recessed fixtures.

To avoid this very real fire hazard, you must install fixtures that are insulated and rated to handle temperatures to 150°F. Underrated recessed lights must be surrounded by noncombustible shields that hold insulation and other flammable materials at least 3 inches away. Or you can use type I, C-rated fixtures with thermo-guards.

Front- and back-door lighting
The NEC stipulates that each entrance to a house must be lighted by an exterior fixture. The light does not have to be mounted near the door but must be switched at the door and must illuminate the area around the entrance. For example, a light on a detached garage will qualify, if it is switched from the inside of the house and it illuminates the space between the garage and house.

Other lighting considerations
As mentioned in the "Switches" section of this chapter, any time a ceiling light is over a stair or in a large room with two entrances, a three-way switch should be used. Dual switching locations are also handy in hallways, garages, and in outbuildings with multiple entrances.

If you have a large yard and spend a lot of time in it, you might also consider installing landscape lighting. Whether you are planning receptacle locations or lighting locations, your decisions should be based on your needs. The minimum standards imposed by the NEC are just that: minimum standards. If you need more, install more.

When you know how you will run each circuit, start by installing boxes and drilling holes for the circuit cables. With the boxes mounted and the holes drilled, start pulling cable through the holes, one circuit at a time.

Because you will have many cables hanging near your panel when it comes time to install the breakers, you should design some method of keeping them straight as you go. The best way is to write directly on the sheathing of each cable with a ballpoint pen. Each wire hanging near the panel will represent a circuit serving a given area of the house. Write "#1 kitchen" on the first of two kitchen appliance circuits, for example. A professional electrician can walk up to a tangle of cables and somehow make sense of them. To the rest of us, however, a dozen unmarked cables looks much more like a can of worms.

Where to run circuit cables

As mentioned earlier, often the most efficient route for you to run cable is right down the center of the house. This will not be true of circuits near the panel, of course, but for those circuits serving the far end of the house, a trunk-line approach is often the easiest. Start by drilling a slightly larger hole than usual, say ⅞ inch in diameter, in each joist near the center beam in the basement. If your home is built on a concrete slab, go through the attic. Then pull three cables through that single row of holes.

As you near each circuit's service location, route a cable to the first outlet box on that circuit. From there, thread a cable through drilled holes in the framed walls or ceiling until all outlets are connected. This trunk-line (with branch runs) approach will help you keep the layout clear in your mind and will also save a lot of unnecessary drilling and pulling.

Mounting the boxes

Receptacle boxes should all be at a uniform height, usually 12 inches from the floor, slightly higher for handicapped users. Switch boxes should be mounted 48 inches from the floor, usually on the door's lock side. Ceiling lights should be centered, or in the case of multiple fixtures, evenly spaced. Install ceiling boxes with brackets to support heavier fixtures or fans.

Where to drill

When threading wire through your home, you should always drill through the framed walls, ceiling joists, and floor joists. Never staple a cable directly across a joist. The exception to this rule is in an attic, and then only near the eaves where there is less than 18 inches between ceiling joists and rafters. If you must lay a cable on top of ceiling joists, nail a furring strip on each side of the cable to protect it. The cable should not be in the open where it could be stepped on or caught by a foot.

When drilling holes in joists and studs, do everything you can to protect the wire and the structure. Always drill through the center of a 2 x 4 stud. When you must drill closer to the edge of a stud than 1¼ inch, nail a ¹⁄₁₆-inch metal plate over the face of the stud to keep from nailing into the cable later. When drilling floor or ceiling joists, drill only in the center one-third of the board. If you drill near the bottom of a joist, you will weaken it. If your new home has floor trusses instead of joists, drill through the plywood center of the trusses and never through the bottom or top rails.

Once you branch off from the trunk, take the most direct route possible. Drill through bottom wall plates and floor decking and pull the cable into the framed walls. From there, drill through each stud on your way to the outlet boxes. Drill these holes at a comfortable height, between 2 and 3 feet from the floor.

If you come to a door frame, drill above it, either through the short studs above the header or through the ceiling joists. Then travel back down and through the studs again. When you come to a framed corner with several thicknesses of 2 x 4s, drop down into the basement until you make it past the corner and then come back up into the wall.

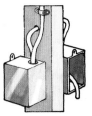

Wiring into boxes
Before bringing cable into metal boxes, you will have to pry one or more knockouts from each box. These knockouts have slots that allow you to twist them out with a screwdriver. Nonmetallic boxes have molded knockout areas that are very thin. To create an opening for a cable, force a screwdriver through the knockout area.

Stapling cables to studs and joists
Any time you run cable along the side of a stud or joist, you must staple it, at least once every 4 feet. The NEC also requires that any cable that enters a box must be stapled within 8 inches of the box. The exception to this rule is when fishing cable into cut-in boxes on remodeling projects, where studs and joists cannot be reached. In these cases, boxes with cable connection clamps must be used.

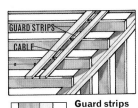

BOX MOUNTED IN FRAMING   SWITCH BOX 4' FROM FLOOR   RECEPTACLE BOX 12" FROM FLOOR

GUARD STRIPS
CABLE

Guard strips
When you must run cable across ceiling joists, protect it with guard strips.

¹⁄₁₆" PLATE

Metal protection plates
Use when wire is within 1¼ inch of the face of a stud.

The service panel

Whether you are wiring a new home or a new addition, you are likely to start in the panel. For the purpose of completeness, we will assume a new panel that is empty and de-energized. How you lay out your new panel, that is, in what order you install the new breakers, is really up to you. Electricians usually install the heavy-duty circuits at the top of the hot bus, just below the main disconnect. An average home might have three 240-volt breakers at the top, followed by six to ten 120-volt breakers below them for the kitchen-appliance circuits and general power circuits.

Connecting circuit breakers

Two-hundred-forty-volt breakers

Practically speaking, a 240-volt circuit is two 120-volt circuits tied together in a panel and at a receptacle.

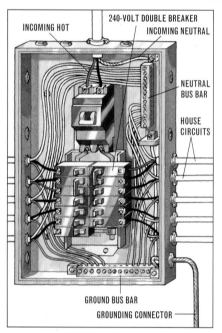

INCOMING HOT

240-VOLT DOUBLE BREAKER
INCOMING NEUTRAL

NEUTRAL
BUS BAR

HOUSE
CIRCUITS

GROUND BUS BAR
GROUNDING CONNECTOR

Circuit cables exiting the sides of the panel
They could also exit the few knockouts at the top.

But technically, there is much more to it. A 240-volt circuit does draw power from two 120-volt circuits, but those circuits are from different phases of a transformer and are of opposite polarity. Transformers have three phases, but today, the third phase is reserved for commercial applications. Appliances requiring 240 volts are wired to draw from two phases through two hot wires.

Your 240-volt cables will each contain one red wire, one black wire, one white wire, and usually one green or bare ground wire. As in 120-volt cables, the white wire will be neutral and the black and red wires hot.

Start by making sure that the main disconnect is shut off. Then insert the cable through one of the panel knockouts and fasten it with a cable connector. Strip off all but ½ inch of the cable's sheathing inside the panel. Then fasten the white wire and the ground wire to the neutral bus bar.

Fasten the black wire to one of the two terminals on the breaker. Follow by fastening the red wire to the other breaker terminal. With the hot wires connected, move the breaker into position on the hot bus. Tip one edge of the breaker under the small retainer on the bus and press the other end onto the two copper tabs projecting from the bus. The breaker should snap firmly in place. Different manufacturers will have slightly different breaker/bus connections.

One-hundred-twenty-volt breakers

Ordinary 120-volt breakers snap into place just like 240-volt breakers. The main difference is that a 120-volt breaker will take up only one breaker slot and cover only one copper tab. Remember that each wire size must be matched to a compatible breaker-amp rating.

Bring a 120-volt cable into another of the panel knockouts. If you have many circuits, you may wish to bring several cables into the panel through the same knockout opening. In that case, wait to tighten the cable connector until all wires are installed. Strip the sheathing from the cable and connect the white neutral and bare ground wires to the neutral bus bar. (If a separate grounding bus is available, ground to it.) Then fasten the black wire to the single breaker terminal.

Grounding the panel

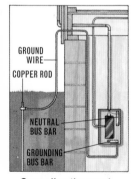

GROUND
WIRE

COPPER ROD

NEUTRAL
BUS BAR

GROUNDING
BUS BAR

Grounding the panel
A service panel must be grounded or its circuit grounding conductors will not be effective.

Just as every neutral and ground wire must be tied to the panel's bus bar, the bus must be connected to a grounding electrode. The electrode, a heavy bare wire, must be fastened to a buried metal surface.

How you connect your system's grounding electrode will depend upon local code requirements. The most common connection is to a metal plumbing system. Other codes require a grounding electrode to be clamped to a ½-inch x 8-foot grounding rod as well as to metal plumbing pipes.

If you fasten your grounding electrode to the plumbing system, make sure that you use approved

clamps. The NEC also requires that you bond a grounding electrode to both sides of the water meter, to circumvent any rubber washers or plastic components that might have been used when the meter was installed.

If you fasten your grounding electrode to a grounding rod, try to drive the rod into the ground at least 8 feet from a basement wall. While the NEC allows grounding rods next to basement walls, it is better to locate them farther away. A grounded charge is dispersed in the soil in a V-shaped pattern, and a wall can reduce the rod's effectiveness.

New wiring in older homes

Drilling top and bottom plates

The trick to electrical remodeling is to work past structural barriers in an inconspicuous way. A few specialized tools will be useful—fish tapes, sabre saws, and extension bits make reaching into blind spaces and blocked passages a lot easier. But a good understanding of how your home was built is your best help. Consider how wall studs and floor and ceiling joists are laid out. Look for nail patterns that suggest the location of a framing member. Check out your basement and attic to determine which way joists run and how far apart they are. As a general rule, walls, floors, and ceilings are laid out on 16-inch centers, that is, framing members are 16 inches apart. Ceiling joists may also be laid out on 24-inch centers. These measurements are standard references, but every home has exceptions. Joists, for example, will often be doubled up for support under walls; corners, doors, windows, and intersecting walls all require extra studs.

Locating studs and fire blocks

The easiest and most certain way to locate obstructions behind plaster or drywall is to buy an electronic density sensor. Unlike magnetic stud finders that react when near nails, density sensors actually sense the extra density of a stud, joist, or fire block and pinpoint the exact edges of a framing member. They also work well through metal lath walls, where magnetic sensors are helpless. You can buy a density sensor at hardware stores and home centers.

You can also locate most studs and fire blocks by visual inspection or by tapping on the wall with your knuckles and listening to its resonance. A hollow sound suggests a hollow space between studs. A dull sound suggests the presence of a stud. To check for fire blocks (short 2 x 4 blocks nailed between studs to stop the spread of fire through wall cavities), rap every few inches between studs in a line between the floor and ceiling. A sudden dull sound between studs indicates a blockage.

Another easy way to locate studs is by looking for nail holes in baseboards. Baseboard nail holes are usually covered with filler that is noticeable at close range. Always look to the nails at the top of the board for clues. The nails at the bottom may be driven into the bottom plate of the wall, which is continuous and therefore deceiving. With a little close inspection, you will be able to predict where most studs and joists are likely to be.

The best places to run wiring are unfinished basement ceilings or unfinished attics. If you have either, make all of your long runs there and wire into the wall only to connect switches or receptacles. In many cases, you will have to go from the basement to the attic at least once. If you have a two-story home, you may have to cut into walls at several levels.

If you have a single-story home, however, getting from the basement to the attic can be as simple as drilling through the top and bottom plates of a center wall and fishing wire from one level to another. The secret to this and all remodeling work is accurate measuring. You will be able to see the top plate in the attic because the ceiling joists will be resting on it. In the basement, however, all you may see are the tips of nails showing through from the bottom plate. You may not see even that much. If not, you will have to measure for the exact location from an outside wall. Measure from the upstairs center wall to an outside wall and transfer that measurement to the basement.

If structural barriers make measuring too difficult, drive a long nail straight down, right next to the wall from upstairs. Then go in the basement and try to locate where the nail broke through the decking. Measure over 3 inches from the nail and drill straight up into the wall.

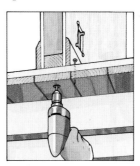

Drill hole into bottom plate using nail as guide

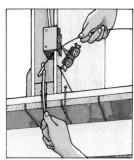

Hook fish tape onto cable and pull up into box

Attach cable to end of fish tape that comes from attic and pull up.

When both top and bottom plates are drilled, slide a fish tape into the wall cavity from each and hook one with the other. Pull the bottom tape down until the end of the tape from the attic is exposed. Attach a cable to the attic tape and pull the tape and cable up through the wall and into the attic.

Pulling wire with fish tape

Fish tapes are the workhorse tools of retrofit wiring. With them, you can reach into closed areas behind walls, ceilings, and floors and pull new wire into otherwise inaccessible places. They are simple to use. You just drill into a wall or joist space and slide the tape along until you can reach it at another location. You can then tie cable to the end of the tape and pull it back through.

In blind spots, you can slide two fish tapes into a space, one from each end. With a little maneuvering, you will be able to hook one tape with the other, giving you the choice of pulling wire from either direction. When working from above, where gravity is a factor in your favor, a small chain offers another option. Your home will dictate the method of use.

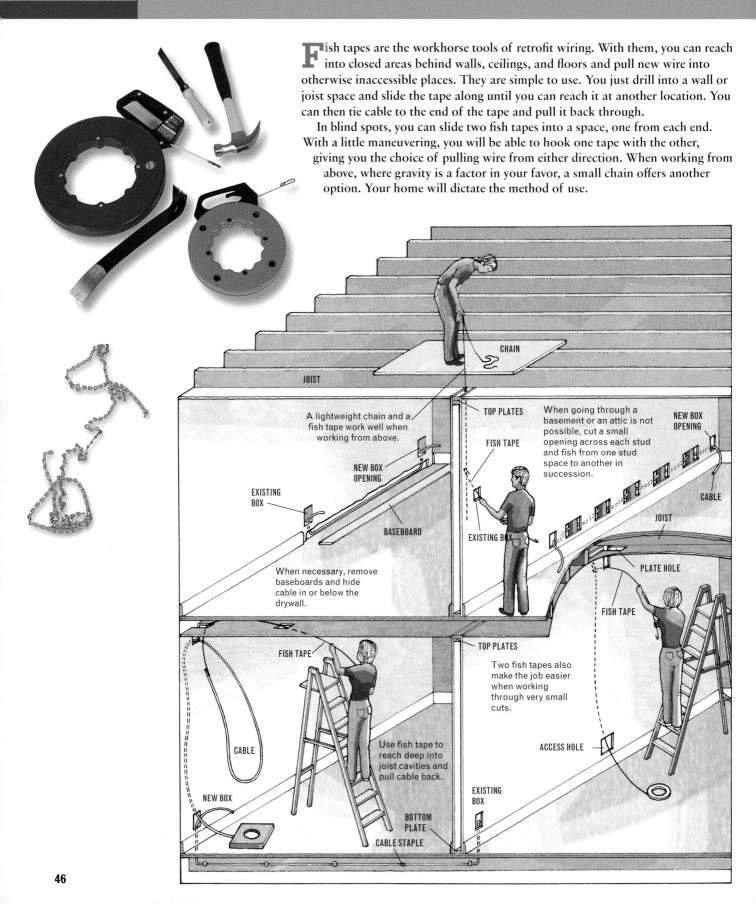

CHAIN

JOIST

A lightweight chain and a fish tape work well when working from above.

TOP PLATES

FISH TAPE

When going through a basement or an attic is not possible, cut a small opening across each stud and fish from one stud space to another in succession.

NEW BOX OPENING

NEW BOX OPENING

EXISTING BOX

CABLE

EXISTING BOX

JOIST

BASEBOARD

PLATE HOLE

When necessary, remove baseboards and hide cable in or below the drywall.

FISH TAPE

FISH TAPE

TOP PLATES

Two fish tapes also make the job easier when working through very small cuts.

CABLE

Use fish tape to reach deep into joist cavities and pull cable back.

ACCESS HOLE

NEW BOX

EXISTING BOX

BOTTOM PLATE

CABLE STAPLE

Running cable under floors

Hiding cable behind woodwork

As you survey your home for possible electrical upgrades, you will see that many changes could be made if you could only get cable from one wall to another. Fortunately, the problem is old enough to have a solution. All it will take is two fish tapes, common household tools, a little planning, and a lot of patience.

Begin with the basics. Make sure that the circuit you want to expand can handle more outlets. Decide which existing outlet offers the easiest tie-in location. Then consider the best route to the new outlet location.

Start by shutting off the power to the circuit you will be tapping. Then remove the coverplate and receptacle from the tie-in box to make sure the circuit is grounded and the wiring is what you expected. For example, is it a middle-of-the-run or an end-of-the-run receptacle? While you are at it, remove a knockout from the bottom of the box for the new cable to come through.

When the existing box is ready, cut the box opening in the new location across the room (see page 48). Then go into the basement and drill up into both walls below each box location. Use a ⅝-inch bit and stay near the center of the wall to avoid drilling into drywall or baseboard nails.

Slide one fish tape through the knockout in the existing box and another tape through the hole drilled from the basement **(1)**. You will need help at this point, but the object is to hook one tape with the other. When you hook them together inside the wall, pull the lower tape up and into the box. Fasten cable to the lower tape **(2)** and pull wire back into the basement and across the floor **(3)**. Then cut the cable so that it will reach well into the new box and push it up into the wall. Have someone reach into the new box opening and pull the wire into the room. Then staple the cable to the floor joists. Slide the cable into the new box and mount the box in the wall. Finally, wire the receptacles and install the coverplates.

If you merely need to run wire down a wall or to the other side of a door but can't get there from an unfinished attic or basement, consider removing a little woodwork and hiding the cable there. The most exacting part of this installation is removing baseboards or trim without damaging them. Use a flat pry bar and a small block of wood to pry against. Push the pry bar behind the trim and gently pry against the block, which you place against the wall. Pry a little at a time from several locations until the trim comes loose. Then carefully pull out the nails from the back side of the board using locking pliers. This will prevent the outside surface of the trim from being damaged.

If the drywall is held up from the floor ½ inch, as it often is, tuck the cable under the drywall. If you do not find a gap under the drywall, use a chisel to cut a small channel for the cable so the trim will fit flat over it. When you renail the trim, be sure to keep the nails above the cable location.

When hiding cable behind door trim, tuck it between the frame and the jamb. If the cable will not fit, you may have to chisel into the drywall or plaster. In either case, staple the cable in place as often as the situation allows. When you reach the box location, drill into the wall behind the trim and run the cable to the opening from inside the wall.

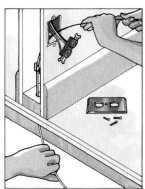

1 Use two fish tapes to pull new wire into existing boxes.

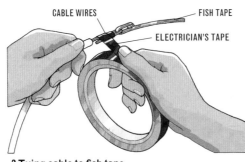

CABLE WIRES — FISH TAPE
— ELECTRICIAN'S TAPE

2 Tying cable to fish tape

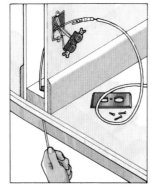

3 Pull the fish tape into the basement with cable attached.

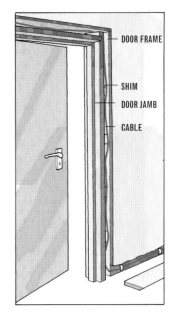

DOOR FRAME
SHIM
DOOR JAMB
CABLE

Installing cut-in boxes

Cut-in boxes are used to upgrade older electrical systems. Unlike standard boxes used in new construction, which are fastened to studs or joists, cut-in boxes are mounted directly to plaster or drywall. They come in several styles with different clamping methods (see page 33). Some have sheet metal spring clamps on the sides, while others have wing nuts or expansion clamps.

The kind you choose is less critical than how you mount it. In each case, the opening must be custom fit to the box's dimensions and characteristics. And of course, what the wall is made of has a lot to do with how you proceed.

Cutting wood lath

Cutting into plaster and wood lath is really not much different from cutting into metal lath. The main difference is that wood is usually easier to cut than metal. You will find the cuts on one side of the opening relatively easy. This is because the lath is still supported from both directions. Once you cut through one side, however, the lath may vibrate too much when you cut it again. If it vibrates too much or tends to spring back when you cut, try a slightly different angle, speed, or pressure. You can usually find a way by making minor adjustments in your approach.

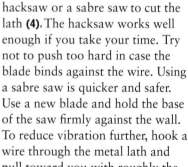

Keyhole saw

Cutting into drywall

Drywall is the easiest of the common wall finishes to cut. It's thin and resonant, which makes finding (and avoiding) studs, joists, or fire blocks easy. It also reveals slight nail depressions, which are usually visible with bright sidelight from a bare bulb. Use a drywall saw, keyhole saw, or utility knife to make the cut.

When using a utility knife, make sure the blade is sharp. Cut the paper all the way around first to set the perimeter, then work the blade deeper with each subsequent cut. Cut in downward strokes with steady, even pressure.

Drywall saw

Cutting into metal lath and plaster

Plaster-covered metal lath can be the trickiest kind of wall finish to cut. The problem is that the expanded metal base that holds the plaster will flex if you try to chisel or saw into it. Too much flexing will cause the wall to crack and can cause the plaster to release from the lath.

Installing cut-in boxes into metal lath requires care, but it can be done with very few special tools. Patience is the key here. Start by locating the studs in the area where you would like your new box. If you do not own a stud finder, rap on the wall to see if you can hear any variation in tone. Where the tone sounds most resonant, pick the spot for your new box.

Before making a cut, drill a very small hole through the plaster and metal lath. Spend a little time reaming the back side of the plaster out with the drill bit. Then bend about 2 inches of a thin wire at a 90-degree angle. Slide the bent part of the wire into the drilled hole and spin it **(1)**. If the wire hits a stud, move to the right or left accordingly. When the bent part of the wire spins all the way around without hitting anything, make your cut.

Before cutting into the plaster, cover the box area with masking tape. This will reinforce the plaster and keep it from chipping during the cut. Then hold the cut-in box,

or its paper template, up to the tape and trace around it **(2)**. With the shape of the box established, drill four holes in the wall, one at each corner of the box. Then use a sharp utility knife to cut into the plaster **(3)**. Do not try to cut all the way through in one slice. Cut a little at a time until you reach the metal lath. Then make several smaller cuts across the section to be removed so that it will come out more easily.

With the plaster cut, use a sharp chisel that you don't mind getting dull to cut and pry the plaster square from the metal. Don't vibrate the lath too much. Just chip a little at a time, in a downward motion. Never tap the chisel straight back toward the lath.

With the plaster out, use a hacksaw or a sabre saw to cut the lath **(4)**. The hacksaw works well enough if you take your time. Try not to push too hard in case the blade binds against the wire. Using a sabre saw is quicker and safer. Use a new blade and hold the base of the saw firmly against the wall. To reduce vibration further, hook a wire through the metal lath and pull toward you with roughly the same pressure you use against the sabre saw. This will steady the saw and the lath. Cut all sides slowly and consistently until the lath drops out.

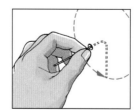

1 Check for blockage by inserting bent wire

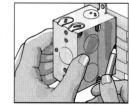

2 Trace around old-work box

3 Use a sharp utility knife to cut plaster

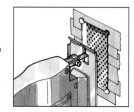

4 Use a sabre saw to cut metal lath

Installing a ceiling box

I f you would like a ceiling light fixture or a ceiling fan added to a room but are put off by the prospect of cutting a hole for a new box into your finished ceiling, don't worry. In most cases the damage caused by ceiling installations is minimal and easy to repair. The hardest part of the job is usually installing the box. As always, the design of your home will determine just how much trouble installing a ceiling fixture will be.

Working from above

If you live in a single-story home with an accessible attic, installing a ceiling box and running wire to it will be easy. Start by deciding exactly where you would like the fixture located. Then drill a small pilot hole in the ceiling from below. Insert a wire about a foot long through the pilot hole so you can see it sticking above the insulation in the attic.

When you find the wire in the attic, make sure there's room for a box and its bracket between joists. If there is, then hold the box up to the ceiling, centered over the pilot hole, and trace around it with a pencil. Cut the hole.

Working through floors

In some cases, working through a second-story floor is easier than cutting into a first-floor ceiling. Floors can be easier to repair, especially when they are covered with rugs. Of course, accurate measurements are a must.

Most homes have two layers of flooring: subflooring and finished flooring. To cut through both layers, make two neat crosscuts, preferably over the top of two joists. Then make two more cuts perpendicular to the

first cuts. Remove any visible nails keeping the cut boards in place. Then, use a chisel or a flat pry bar to pry the flooring away from the joists and lift the boards up.

Working from below

If fine hardwood floors or a flat roof prevent you from working from above, you may have to cut into the ceiling from below. While this will require some plaster or drywall repair, you should not let it get in the way of your lighting needs. Such repairs are straightforward and can be learned in short order.

If you need to cut into the ceiling from below, make a big enough access hole to fit a standard bracket box (or an NEC-approved fan box) and a 2 x 4 nailer. A large hole will make fishing cable to a power source or switch a lot easier. And a large hole is no harder to repair than a small one.

The wiring method you use to bring power into the ceiling box will depend on the location of the most convenient power source, and whether you want to control the fixture from one or two locations.

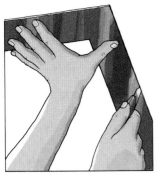
Making a square opening
Use a framing square to draw a square opening. The opening will be easier to repair if it is uniform.

Replacing the drywall piece
You can often use the same square of drywall you cut out to cover the hole.

Choosing a ceiling box

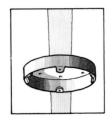

The kind of ceiling box you buy will depend upon the access you have to the ceiling joists and the kind of fixture you wish to install. If you have access to joists from above or if you have no access and must cut an access hole in the drywall or plaster, then a bracket box is your best choice. Bracket boxes give the best support. If you are installing a lightweight ceiling fixture, a cut-in box or a pancake box will do the job. A pancake box should be used only in an end-of-the-run installation because the box area is too small to contain more wires.

The NEC specifies that paddle-type ceiling fans must be installed in specially approved ceiling boxes. If a box conforms to this NEC standard it will be stamped accordingly. To give yourself even more protection, you should bolt these boxes to 2 x 4 blocks nailed between joists.

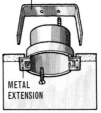

Cut-in box
For lightweight ceiling fixtures only, never for ceiling fans.

Pancake box
For end-of-circuit use where only one cable will be in the box.

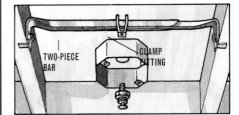
Clamp fittings on bracket boxes

Extending existing circuits

A junction box—basically a box covered with a plate—is used to house and protect wire connections made between outlet boxes and must remain accessible at all times. Wire connections must never be made outside a box, even if hidden in an attic or crawl space.

Installing a new junction box

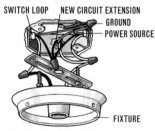

1 Extending a circuit from a new junction box

You will sometimes have the amp capacity to add fixtures or outlets, but doing so will require cutting into the middle of a circuit. A case in point would be when the easiest and most economical tie-in location is in the attic and not near receptacle or light fixture boxes.

Start by shutting off power to the circuit. Then mount a round or octagonal box on an attic ceiling joist right next to the circuit cable **(1)**. Cut the cable and pull as much slack out of it from each direction as you can. This will give you longer leads to work with in the box. Then bring both ends of the existing circuit and the new branch cable into

the box. Secure each cable with a cable connector or staple them within 8 inches of the box.

Assuming you already have the add-on boxes wired, you will now be ready to tie the new branch line into the existing circuit. To make this connection, join each color-coded set of wires in the box with a wire connector. To ground a metal junction box, run a pigtail from the ground wires to the box screw. In plastic boxes, just join all the ground wires in a wire connector.

Finally, cover the box with a blank plate and restore power. The plate of the box must remain accessible, so don't cover it up.

Converting an existing box

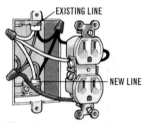

2 Running a new circuit from an end-of-the-run receptacle

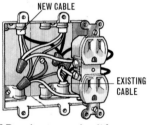

3 Running a new circuit from an expanded middle-of-the-run receptacle

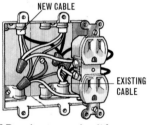

4 Extending circuit from an overhead fixture

Often a receptacle box can serve as a junction box while also serving its original purpose. (The same applies to ceiling boxes if they are not end-of-run outlets.) Technically, these boxes are not junction boxes because they still hold receptacles or fixtures, but whenever possible, use them as junction boxes. Junction boxes are always in danger of being covered up by someone in the future. Ceiling and receptacle boxes generally are not.

End-of-the-run junctions
To add a circuit branch from a receptacle used as a junction box, try to find the last receptacle on the existing circuit. Because it will have only two existing wires, you will not be exceeding the NEC's allowable number of wires per box. You also won't have to worry about interrupting receptacles down the line.

Shut off the power and bring the new cable into the end-of-the-run box. Remove the wires from the receptacle and tie each set of corresponding wires together with pigtails. Connect the loose ends of the pigtails to opposing receptacle terminals **(2)**. Replace the coverplate.

Middle-of-the-run junctions
Middle-of-the-run receptacles are trickier, because by adding two more wires and a ground, you exceed the number of wires the NEC allows for a small box. You will have to install a larger cut-in box or add a box extension **(3)**. (The latter is possible only if the existing box is expandable.) Choose the method that makes the job easiest.

Once the box size has been fixed, bring the new branch cable into the box. Join all corresponding wires with wire connectors and pigtail the joined black and white wires to the original receptacle terminals. Join all the ground wires and a grounding pigtail with a wire contractor. Attach the other end of the pigtail to the grounding screw in the back of the box. Finally, cover the receptacle and restore power to the circuit.

Ceiling box junctions
If a ceiling box is served by a cable that's hot all the time instead of just a switch leg, it can be used easily as a junction box. Sometimes ceiling fixtures wired in this manner are switched by a pull chain, and at other times they are connected to a switch loop. When tapping into a fixture operated by a pull chain, just tie all corresponding wires together in the box with wire connectors and pigtail from the wires to the original fixture terminals **(4)**.

When tapping into a box with a hot cable and a switch loop, start by cutting the white wire from the incoming power cable that leads to the fixture. Then use a wire connector to join the white wire from the extension to the two wires produced by the cut. Next, join the black wires from the power source, the extension circuit, and the switch with a wire connector. Then join the white wire from the switch to the other fixture lead with a wire connector. Connect all the ground wires and attach them to the box with a pigtail.

Surface wiring

If cutting into finished walls, ceilings, and floors is more than you feel like taking on, consider making electrical improvements out in the open, through raceways. Surface wiring kits have been popular for years, for just this reason. Because surface wiring adds to the cost of the job, plan carefully to avoid buying unnecessary parts or making wrong cuts.

Tapping into existing receptacles

The advantage of surface wiring is that you can tap into an existing receptacle without cutting into the wall. This is accomplished by an extension adapter. The adapter fits over an existing box, and the wires from the raceway are joined to the receptacle wires with pigtails to continue the circuit.

To install this adapter, shut off the power to the circuit and remove the coverplate from the box. Pull out the receptacle and screw the adapter plate to the box. Break out the slot you need in the raceway-extension frame box to accommodate the raceway channel. Then place the extension frame over the channel and snap it onto the adapter plate.

To connect the wires, start by making four 5-inch pigtail wires, one black, one white, and two green. Join the incoming-power black wire to the black raceway wire and the black pigtail inside a wire connector. Then tie the other end of the black pigtail to the hot side of the receptacle. In like manner, join all white wires and pigtail them to the neutral side of the receptacle.

To properly ground the system, attach one pigtail to the grounding screw on the receptacle and the other pigtail to the grounding screw at the back of the box. Then join both pigtails and the grounding wire from the power line and from the raceway with a wire connector.

Fasten the receptacle to the extension frame with screws and replace the coverplate.

Begin installation by mounting all base channels and box base plates on wall and ceiling.

Place all wires in base channel, then carefully snap trim channel over all base channels.

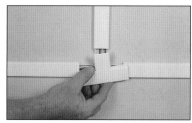
Finish all trim channel joints with a variety of trim connecting pieces.

Raceways come in pieces that you assemble to fit your needs. A raceway consists of a base channel and a trim channel that together form a small rectangular tube that carries the circuit wires. The base channel screws directly to walls or ceiling. Once the wires are in place, the trim snaps over the base channel. To cover in-line joints, small cover clips are provided. A variety of elbow and tee clips are used when turning corners and changing directions.

When installing raceways, first screw all the base channels and electrical-box baseplates to the walls and ceiling. Then lay the wires into the base channels and hold the wires in place with wire clips. Carefully measure the lengths of the trim channel pieces. Cut them and snap them in place. Then add any connecting pieces that are necessary, mount the boxes, and install the receptacles, switches, and light fixtures the job requires.

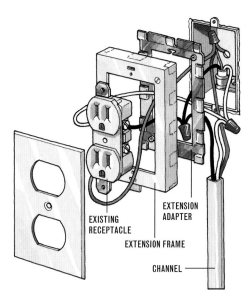

EXISTING RECEPTACLE

EXTENSION ADAPTER

EXTENSION FRAME

CHANNEL

Attach an extension frame to ceiling-fixture base plate with screws.

Join fixture leads to raceway wire with wire connectors then screw fixture to extension frame.

Wiring 240-volt appliances

The major appliances that use 240-volt circuits make our lives a lot easier. Electric clothes dryers, water heaters, and air conditioners have become indispensible components of our comfortable lives. If you need another 240-volt appliance and your service panel has the space and the amperage to handle it, don't let working with 240 volts scare you. In some ways, 240-volt circuits are safer than 120-volt circuits because the amperage is split between two conductors.

If you can wire a 120-volt circuit, you already have the skills to wire a 240-volt circuit. For all practical purposes, 240-volt circuits are just two 120-volt circuits tied together. In actuality, this is not so because each 120 volts comes from a separate phase of a transformer. But when you run wires and hook up breakers and receptacles, there isn't much difference in the basic technique.

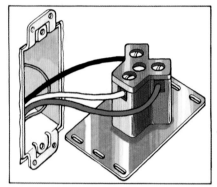

A wall-mounted 120/240 receptacle

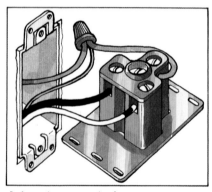

A dryer-type receptacle

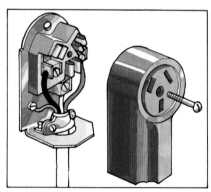

A range-type receptacle

Two-wire and three-wire receptacles

It won't take you long to discover that the receptacle for your electric range does not look the same as the one for your electric clothes dryer. For one thing, the socket holes are different. You can't plug a range into a dryer receptacle, or vice versa. These variations may seem superficial, but they are the electrical industry's gentle way of telling you there is a major difference in how 240-volt circuits are wired.

The main difference is that some 240-volt appliances, such as air conditioners, water heaters, and dryers, need 240 volts only. Other appliances, like electric ranges, need both a 240-volt and a 120-volt circuit in a single receptacle. A range, for example, requires 240 volts for high heat but might require only 120 volts for lower settings. And any built-in timers or lights would use only 120 volts. As you can see, the needs of the appliance involved affect how many wires a circuit should have

and therefore which receptacle you must use.

A 240-volt, dryer-type receptacle needs only two wires and a ground to complete its circuit. In this case, a black wire and a white or red wire are brought into a three-terminal receptacle. The two hot wires are connected to the two hot terminals. The ground wire from the service panel is attached to a pigtail from the receptacle and a pigtail to the grounding screw at the back of the box. This is all there is to wiring a two-wire, 240-volt dryer receptacle.

Because other 240-volt appliances require a 120-volt circuit to function properly, an extra wire from the cable is needed. In these cases, the cable carries black and red hot wires, a white neutral wire, and a ground wire. Large room air conditioners are usually plugged into wall-mounted receptacles. But electric ranges have a specific box and plug.

Wiring at subpanel

The neutral bus bar in a subpanel is never bonded directly to the panel when 240-volt circuits are involved. It is attached only through nonconducting spacers. If the neutral wire were bonded directly to a subpanel, it would divide the circuit so that the breaker would read only half of a potential overload, thereby creating a fire hazard. Because of this, when running a 240-volt circuit through a subpanel, four wires must be used. The neutral wire from the 240-volt circuit should travel uninterrupted to the main-panel neutral bus bar. The ground wire, on the other hand, must be bonded to the grounding bus in both the subpanel and the main panel.

Installing a 240-volt breaker

To install a 240-volt breaker, shut off the main disconnect breaker and bring the circuit cable into the panel. Fasten it with a cable connector. Then strip the sheathing from all but about ½ inch of the cable, and bond the ground and neutral wires to the neutral bus bar. Connect the black wire to one breaker terminal and the red wire to the other. Push the breaker into the hot bus bar. Replace the panel cover, turn on the main disconnect breaker, and turn on the 240-volt circuit breaker.

A 240-volt breaker has two terminal screws; attach red hot wire to one and black hot wire to the other.

Once circuit wires are attached to the breaker, push breaker into hot bus bar.

Running 240-volt cables

Heavy-duty circuits require heavy wire, such as No. 10 or No. 8. When several of these thick wires are contained in a single cable, that cable is very stiff. In some situations, it is too stiff to be pulled through drilled joists and studs. To accommodate this problem, some code authorities allow No. 8 cable to be strapped or stapled directly to unfinished joists or to the sides of 2 x 4 running boards nailed to open joists. Others disallow any surface-mounted cable and require that any wire too stiff to pull through the framing must be run inside conduit. Any drop from ceiling to appliance should also be encased in conduit.

Wiring to 120-volt appliances

While fixed appliances like dishwashers, trash compactors, and garbage disposers are sometimes found on kitchen-appliance circuits, they should have their own circuits. So should refrigerators. The same is true of microwave ovens, because they create voltage irregularities in a wiring system, and of computers, because they can be sensitive to voltage irregularities. Many older homes, however, do not have enough room in their service panels for so many circuits. If you are working against such limitations, follow the NEC's minimum standards and do the best you can. The NEC allows a fixed appliance to be plugged into an outlet only when it has a factory-installed cord with a grounded plug. In some situations, a dishwasher and a disposer can share a circuit, but dedicated circuits are preferable.

Wiring a garbage disposer

To install a disposer in a sink that has not previously had one, you will have to bring power to a new switch nearby and then into the sink cabinet. A 14/2 cable with ground will give you the number of wires and amperage you need.

Start in the panel to make sure you have the expansion room for another appliance. The first step is to bring cable from the panel to the wall behind the sink. If the basement is open, run cable from the panel to the sink wall and drill up through the bottom wall plate. If there's no basement, approach the job from the attic. Run the cable directly to the sink area and fish down into the wall cavity through the wall's top plate.

Next, cut a hole for a cut-in box in the sink wall and pull the cable through this hole. Then fish a second cable from the sink cabinet to the box opening. With both wires through the hole, slide them into the box and mount the box in the wall. Tie the neutral wires together with a wire connector in the box, and fasten a black wire to each terminal on a single-pole switch. Then join the ground wires and a grounding pigtail together with a wire connector and attach the pigtail to the grounding screw at the back of the box. Attach the switch to the box and install a coverplate.

With the switch installed, go into the sink cabinet and slide

flexible metal conduit over the cable from the disposer to the wall. The conduit should stick through the wall a little and be fastened to the disposer with a conduit connector. Inside the disposer housing, you will find a black stranded wire, a white stranded wire, and a ground screw. Attach the cable's ground wire to the ground screw. Use wire connectors to join the black cable wire and the black disposer lead. Join the white wires the same way. Fold the wires and connectors into the disposer housing and fasten the coverplate over the opening. Hang the unit from the bottom of the sink, install a 20-amp breaker in the service panel, and test the disposer.

Install a conduit connector on the bottom of the disposer, then attach flexible conduit.

Wiring a dishwasher

Join like-colored wires with wire connectors and attach ground wire to disposer grounding screw.

Dishwashers and disposers are wired in similar ways, except that a dishwasher does not need an external switch. Start by bringing 14/2 with ground cable through the wall or floor of the dishwasher cabinet. Because the cable will be hidden under the dishwasher and out of reach, you will not need to encase it in flexible conduit. Simply bring it into the cabinet space so that it is long enough to reach the front of the dishwasher. Slide the dishwasher into place, level the legs, and secure its brackets to the countertop. Then remove the

access panel and complete the plumbing connections.

With everything else connected, remove the plate from the electrical box containing the lead wires. Bring the stripped cable into the box and fasten it with a cable connector. Then join the dishwasher leads to the like-colored cable wires with wire connectors. Attach the cable ground wire to the grounding screw in the box. Replace the box cover and the front access panel of the dishwasher. Then install a 20-amp breaker in the service panel.

Install a cable connector in dishwasher electrical box and slide cable through connector.

Join cable wires to dishwasher leads with wire connectors; join ground wire to ground screw.

Attics hold an incredible amount of heat in the summer. Temperatures that can easily exceed 150°F are not much affected by simple louvers and vents. Very high attic temperatures put an extra load on your home's cooling system and, in extreme cases, can damage roofing and plywood sheathing.

The solution is as simple as installing a power-exhaust attic fan. A thermostatically controlled model will make your home more comfortable in summer while protecting your roof and saving you a lot on your cooling bill.

Selecting a fan

An attic fan simply pulls cooler air through soffit and gable vents into the attic and exhausts the hot air to the outside. When shopping for an attic fan, make sure you buy one with a high enough CFM (cubic feet per minute) rating. Your dealer should be able to help you select a size to fit your needs. If you prefer making your own estimates, multiply your attic's square footage by 0.7. The total will give you the CFM rating you need. If your roof shingles are black or very dark, add 10 to 15 percent to the CFM total.

Mounting a fan

Start by going into your attic and locating the best spot to install the fan. Choose a rafter or truss space near the center of your home and about 3 feet down from the peak of the roof, usually on the side opposite the street. Then measure for the center of the space and drill a small pilot hole through the sheathing and shingles from the inside **(1)**.

With the pilot hole made, take a sabre saw, a utility knife, and the fan up on the roof. Center the fan housing over the pilot hole and slide it to a position that requires cutting the fewest number of shingles. The top two-thirds of the flashing on the fan is designed to slide under the shingles and the bottom one-third will fit on top of the shingles. To do this, you may need to slide a hacksaw blade under some of the shingles and cut a few nails.

Mark the top and bottom positions of the flashing lightly with the knife and then set the fan aside. The directions that come with the fan will indicate the size and position of the hole that must be cut in the roof. If your fan comes with a template, use it. Once the correct hole location is established, use a sharp knife to cut the shingles away. With the shingles and roofing felt removed, use a sabre saw to cut through the sheathing **(2)**.

Slide the upper part of the flashing under the shingles. Then carefully lift the shingles and nail the flashing at each side so that the nails are under the shingles. While the bottom of the flashing is still loose, coat the underside with plastic roofing compound. Also coat the underside of any shingles that lie on the flashing. Then nail the bottom of the flashing over the shingles **(3)**.

To get power to the fan, first screw the thermostat to a rafter or truss near the peak. Then run flexible conduit over to the fan motor.

The easiest way to get power to the thermostat is to tap into an existing circuit in the attic either inside a pull-chain light-fixture box or by installing a junction box next to a cable. Shut off power to the circuit you've chosen and bring a 14/2 with ground cable from the thermostat to the fixture or junction box. Inside the box, join like-colored wires with wire connectors.

Return to the thermostat and join the white cable and white fan lead with a wire connector. Do the same with all the ground wires. Then join one lead from the thermostat to the black lead coming from the power source with a wire connector. Join the other thermostat lead to the black wire going to the fan with a wire connector. Put the coverplate on the thermostat box and the junction box, if you installed one. Or reinstall the light fixture if one was used. Turn on the power and check your work.

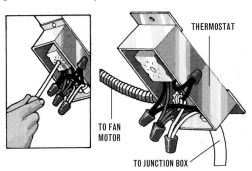

THERMOSTAT

TO FAN MOTOR

TO JUNCTION BOX

Temperature adjustments
Inside the thermostat box, you will see a set screw pointer on a dial. By turning this screw, you set the temperature at which the fan will come on. Try 90°F as a starting temperature. The fan will automatically shut off when the attic temperature drops 10°. If you find that the fan runs continuously, adjust the setting for a little higher startup temperature.

1 Drill up through roof at center of rafter space

2 Cut through roof sheathing with sabre saw

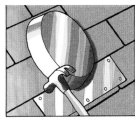

3 Slide fan into place and nail flashing

Installing a bathroom fan

The national Uniform Plumbing Code states that your bathroom must have either a window that opens or an exhaust fan. Even if you have two windows offering cross-ventilation, a fan is a good idea. The reason is that excess moisture causes paint to peel and can cause wood to rot. It warps cabinet doors and can fill a bathroom with mold spores, which are a common cause of allergic reaction.

Exhaust fans come in a variety of styles with a choice of features. A simple exhaust fan is easiest to install and supply with power, but fan/light combinations and fan/heater combinations offer greater utility in a single fixture. In many cases, you will be able to install a fan/light combination in place of an existing overhead light fixture. If your bathroom feels cold when you step out of the tub, a fan/heater combination can help take the chill out of the air.

The kind of fan you choose depends on your needs, but structural factors will play a role, too. If you cannot run a three-wire cable from an existing switch to the fan location without going through a lot of trouble, it might be better to settle for a simple fan or fan/light combination. Plan your wiring before you buy any unit.

FAN UNIT

FLEXIBLE DUCT

Venting the fan

If a bathroom fan is improperly vented, condensation will form and run back into the ceiling, causing stains and ruining drywall. The best way to vent a fan is to connect a flexible plastic dryer vent between the fan and the soffit vent. A dryer vent is easy to cut and bend and slips easily into tight spaces. When in a horizontal position, condensation is not likely to run back into the ceiling.

Another option is to cut a vent into the roof and vent the fan through a vertical exhaust pipe. There are pitfalls to this method. One of them is the flashing. Cutting into an existing roof is always a risk; anything less than a perfect seal will leak. Secondly, with the vent pipe in a vertical position, condensation can run straight back into the fan and ceiling. If you have a choice, vent horizontally to a soffit using either a dryer vent or galvanized sheetmetal pipe and fittings.

Installing a fan switch box

Determine best spot for switch, then trace box onto wall.

Cut box hole and fish cable from fan and power source.

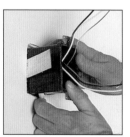

Slide cables into cut-in box and push box into hole.

Fan or fan/light installation

If you use the switch loop from an existing light to control a new fan/light combination, both the fan and the light will go on when you flip the switch. Start by shutting off the power to the circuit and removing the old fixture and ceiling box. Then measure carefully and cut the ceiling to accept the fan housing. Fasten the housing to the ceiling joists and bring the switch wires into the housing. If the fan and light are not factory installed in the housing, install these components and plug each into its receptacle.

Tie the switch wires to the fixture leads with wire connectors and attach the ground wire to the box's grounding screw. Finally, install the light diffuser and decorative cover and restore power to the circuit.

If you want separate fan and light switches, you will have to run a three-wire cable between the switch box and fixture and install a double switch in the switch box. The connection will be similar to that of a three-way switch (see page 36). A common wire will serve both fixture components and two travelers will complete the circuit for each switch.

Fan/light/heater installations

A three-component fixture will require four wires. You can bring these four wires in as 2 two-wire cables or you can run a single length of flexible conduit between the switch and the fixture. In this case, you would pull four separate insulated wires and a ground wire through the conduit.

Either way is code approved, but for most people, running the two cables will be easier. Fortunately, four-wire fixtures usually come with combination switches that control all three operations in one unit. This keeps you from having to install three separate switches in an expanded box.

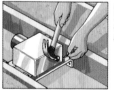

Anchor fan housing into ceiling from above

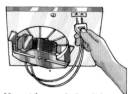

Mount fan and plug it in

Installing a ceiling fan

Reinforcing a ceiling box

I f you're tired of looking at that old, outdated ceiling fixture and you'd prefer a ceiling fan/light combination, don't be intimidated by the prospect of installing one yourself. There are a lot of models to choose from in a wide price range. But all are installed in a similar way.

Many people use these fans to keep a room cool in the summer. But they can be almost as effective for keeping a room warm in the winter by circulating the warm air that tends to hover near the ceiling.

Remove mounting screws to existing light fixture and pull down fixture; remove wires.

Remove insulation from around box and cut 2 x 4 block to fit between joists; nail it into joists.

Drive 1½-inch-long wood screws through fixture box and into support block.

Hanging the fan

Begin by installing the fan mounting plate that comes with the fan. Use 4-inch-long wood screws, and drive them through the mounting plate and the ceiling box into the support block nailed between the joists. Pull the switch wires through the hole in the mounting plate. Then fabricate a short hook from stiff wire and hang it from the plate. This wire must be strong enough to temporarily support the fan when you are making the wiring connections.

Lift the fan assembly onto the hook and join the black wire to the black fixture lead with a wire connector. Do the same with both white wires. Join the two ground wires to a grounding pigtail and attach the pigtail to the grounding screw in the ceiling box.

Remove the temporary support hook and push the fan canopy over the mounting plate. Then screw the canopy to the plate. Because these screws are what hold the fan in place, make sure they are tight. With the fan assembly in place, mount each fan blade on its metal bracket and then mount the brackets on the fan.

If your fan came with a light kit, remove the cap on the bottom of the fan housing to access the light wires. Pull down the white neutral wire and the black hot wire. Next attach the light-kit adapter ring , supplied with the fan, to the fan housing. Lift the light fixture close to the fan and make the wire connections. Join white to white, and black to black, with wire connectors.

Fasten the light fixture to the fan with the screws provided and install vibration-resistant bulbs in the fixture. In most cases, 60-watt bulbs are the maximum you can use. Anything brighter poses a fire hazard.

You need to beef up the support for the ceiling box so it can safely handle the weight of the fan. Code requires either a 2 x 4 brace nailed between joists to support the box, or an approved box with a bracket designed to carry the weight.

Access to the box from above makes a 2 x 4 block the simpler option. Just pull the insulation away from the box, cut a 2 x 4 to fit tightly between the joists, and nail it in place. Then go below and drive 1½-inch-long wood screws through fixture box and into the support block.

If you don't have access from above and must come through the box hole in the room's ceiling, then use the bracket box. These units are designed to fit through a ceiling-box opening. To install one, you first remove the existing box, then insert the circuit wires into the box and push the box with the bracket into the joist cavity. Once in the cavity, you turn the mounting bar from below and sharp prongs are driven into the joist. Installed properly, the bracket can support the fan.

Drive screws through mounting plate and ceiling box into support block until plate is tight to ceiling.

Hang fan assembly from mounting plate and join fan leads to power cable leads.

Attach fan securely to mounting plate, then install fan blades on mounting brackets.

Planning your lighting

To be successful, lighting must allow you to work, read, or study without straining your eyes. It should also brighten areas that are potentially dangerous and provide satisfactory background illumination at all times of the day. With so many needs to fulfill, sometimes the decorative possibilities of lighting are ignored. Good lighting can create an atmosphere of warmth and well-being, highlight objects of interest, transform the character of an interior, and still look good.

Atmospheric lighting (below left)
A subdued, moody feel is created by a combination of candlelight and electric fixtures controlled by dimmer switches.

Task-lighting (below right)
These days, just about every home office is organized around a computer. Some background lighting is required to reduce the strain of staring into a bright monitor, and you need adjustable task-lighting to illuminate the desktop without reflecting in the screen.

Illuminating living rooms

When planning lighting for a living room, the emphasis should be on versatility—creating areas of strong light where it is needed most and areas of subtle light for reading and relaxation. Seating areas are best served by lighting placed at a low level, so that naked bulbs do not shine light directly into your eyes and you're still able to read a book or newspaper in a comfortable chair. Choose lighting that isn't harsh, so it won't cause glare on white paper, and supplement it with low-powered lighting to maintain a suitable level of ambient light in the room.

Working at a desk demands similar conditions, but the light source must be stronger and situated in front of you, to avoid your own shadow being thrown across the work. Choose a properly shaded desk lamp, or conceal lighting under wall storage or bookshelves above the desk.

Similar concealed lighting is ideal for entertainment centers, but you may need extra lighting in the form of ceiling-mounted spotlights to illuminate the shelves themselves. Another good option is track lighting that lets you put any number of light heads on the ceiling so you can shine them wherever you want.

Concealed lighting in other areas of the living room can be very attractive. Strip lights placed on top (and at the back) of high cabinets will bounce light off the ceiling. You can also hide lighting behind window valances to accentuate window treatments, or put it along a wall to illuminate pictures. Individual works of art can be accentuated with a light or two placed above them. Or you can install an adjustable ceiling spotlight that will place a pool of light exactly where you want it. Avoid pointing lamps directly at pictures protected by glass because the reflections will obscure what's behind the glass. Usually, overhead lighting is not used in living rooms because it can be harsh. Wall-mounted sconces work better for general lighting purposes because they reflect softer light off the walls.

Sleeping areas

Bedside lamps or lighting fixtures abovea headboard are basic requirements in any bedroom. Most are simple incandescent units selected more for how they look than how they work. If you and your partner read in bed, equip your lights with dimmer controls operated from the night stand, not the wall. This will allow each of you to adjust the light so it doesn't disturb the other.

A dressing table needs its own light source placed so that it cannot be seen in the mirror but still illuminates the person using it. Wall lights or recessed lights in the ceiling can provide general lighting, but be sure to install them with dimmer switches so you can control the light intensity in the room.

Make sure bedside lamps in a child's room are as tamperproof as possible. A dimmer switch for the main room lighting will provide enough light to comfort a child at night but can be turned to full brightness for evening playtime.

Dining areas and kitchens

Because its height can be adjusted exactly, a pull-down pendant light (or a chandelier on a dimmer switch) is a good choice for lighting over a dining table. If you eat in the kitchen, have separate controls for the table lighting and work areas so you can create a comfortable dining space without having to illuminate the rest of the room. In addition to a good background light, illuminate kitchen countertops with undercabinet lighting and place track lighting or recessed ceiling spotlights over the sink and kitchen island.

Bathrooms

Safety must be your first priority when choosing light fixtures for a bathroom. They have to be designed to withstand moisture-laden air and still last for a long time. Creating subtle lighting in a bathroom is often challenging, but concealed light directed onto the ceiling from a wall valance is one solution. Be sure to provide strong light above or to the sides of a mirror over a lavatory or vanity.

Staircases

Light staircases from above so that the treads are illuminated clearly, throwing the risers into shadow. This will define the steps for anyone with poor eyesight. Place a light over each landing or at the top, bottom, and middle of circular staircases. Three-way switches at the top and bottom of the stairs are essential to ensure that no one has to use the stairs in darkness.

Workshops

Plan workshop lighting with efficiency and safety in mind. Illuminate a fixed workbench the same way as a desk and provide individual, adjustable light fixtures for machine tools. Most people use inexpensive fluorescent fixtures for general workshop lighting. These provide lots of light, are easy to install, and are economical to run. Daylight bulbs that mimic the look of sunlight are available for these units.

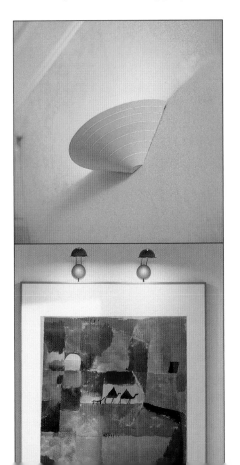

Creating indirect lighting

Where to hide fixtures

Architects are taught to think of lighting not only as a tool of daily living but as a part of a home's design. Today, lighting manufacturers are directing more and more of their energies to fixtures that can create dramatic effects.

Even with all the technical advancements available to you, some of the most creative lighting techniques can still be created with inexpensive fixtures, common materials, and a little imagination. You can change the entire mood of a room by hiding a few lights behind coves and valances and letting them spill soft lighting onto ceilings or down from cabinets. The idea of indirect lighting is not to flood a room with light, but to direct attention toward or away from some feature of a room. If you would like your lighting to do more, consider the indirect approach.

Choosing the right fixtures

Fluorescent fixtures are the most commonly used in indirect lighting. They produce soft white light without glare or hot spots. They also produce very little heat and so can be installed in tight spaces. Fluorescent lights come in a variety of sizes that can be easily adapted to any length of cove, soffit, valance, or ceiling recess.

Wiring indirect lighting

Another advantage of fluorescent fixtures is that they can easily be ganged together and wired in sequence. Just mount the fixtures end-to-end and connect them with insulated jumper wires, black ties to black and white ties to white, just as you would expect. Because the fixture channels are made of metal, all you have to do to ground each fixture is fasten a ground jumper wire to each channel. A continuous ground wire will not be needed. Then tie the last channel to the grounding conductor in the cable. With the fixtures tied together, switch the entire series with a single-pole switch located in a convenient spot.

Installing an undercabinet light

Drill hole in back of cabinet and cut hole in wall for switch; fish cable between the two.

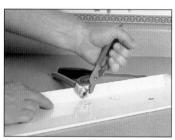

To protect cable until it goes into wall, attach short length of flexible conduit to back of fixture.

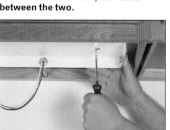

Attach fixture channel to underside of cabinet with one screw at each end.

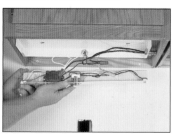

Join switch wires to fixture wires, then mount fixture in channel.

Indirect lighting can be installed anywhere you feel like putting it, provided NEC minimum clearances are observed. The four most common ways to hide indirect lights are behind a cornice board, valance, soffit, or cove. In each case, you will build a trough to hide the fixture. You can be as creative as you wish, but remember to leave enough clearance so that the enclosure is not trapping too much heat and is accessible for maintenance.

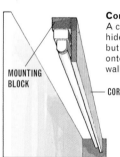

Cornice boards
A cornice board hides the tube, but spills the light onto a nearby wall.

MOUNTING BLOCK

CORNICE BOARD

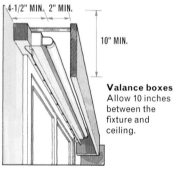

4-1/2" MIN. 2" MIN.

10" MIN.

Valance boxes
Allow 10 inches between the fixture and ceiling.

ANGLE BRACKET

Soffit lights
Over a workspace, use a two-tube light for added brightness.

8" TO 12"

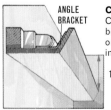

ANGLE BRACKET

Cove lighting
Cove lighting bounces light onto the ceiling, into the room.

10" MIN.

Installing track lighting

Track lighting is one of the most versatile lighting options. In this system individual lamps, or heads as they're called, are attached to tracks mounted on the ceiling. Because the tracks can be installed practically anywhere, you can place them where they'll do the most good. And because the lamps are designed to move along the tracks, you can vary the light intensity in different parts of the room. You can also change the lighting arrangement at the drop of a hat, to accommodate new requirements or just to try something new.

Choosing your lights
The clearest choices in track lighting systems focus on the head design. Some have small, unobtrusive can-shaped heads. Others have large, high-tech lamps that lend drama to a room, even when they're turned off. A quick trip to a lighting showroom will provide you with options that can fit any room and any budget.

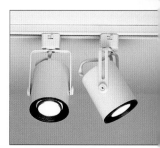

Installing the tracks

First, study the layout of your room and decide on the best placement for your track sections. Plan on the first track to start at an existing light fixture. This will be the power source for the tracks. Keep in mind that all the lamps can be adjusted in any direction to provide general room illumination and specific task lighting.

Start by shutting off the power to the ceiling fixture and removing the fixture from the ceiling box. Remove the existing fixture mounting strap from the box and replace it with the one that came with your system. Then slide a feed connector into the first piece of track.

The track is held to the ceiling with toggle bolts. The toggle bolts require holes in the ceiling that are big enough for the expanding spring clamps to fit through. To locate these holes, hold the track in place and mark the bolt holes on the ceiling. Then remove the track and drill the holes.

Install the toggles in the track holes, hold the track up near the ceiling, and squeeze the spring clips so they can fit through the holes. Tighten the bolts most of the way but leave room for adjustment. Repeat this process for the other tracks. When all are joined, finish tightening all the toggle bolts.

Install connectors in ends of track.

Hang tracks from ceiling with toggle bolts.

Once all tracks are assembled, draw bolts tight.

Wiring and light heads

With all the tracks assembled and secured to the ceiling, attach the wires that power the system. Connect the black and white wires from the ceiling box to the feed connector on the first piece of track. The black wire goes to the brass screw and the white wire goes to the silver screw. Attach the ground wire to the grounding screw on the connector. Push the feed connector cover over the end of the track and the bottom of the ceiling box and attach it.

To install the first lamp, push the top of the fixture into the track with the lamp contacts parallel to the length of the track. Rotate the fixture a quarter of a turn, so its

polarity arrow points to the polarity line on the track. You should hear the lamp click into place. Each lamp has a switch. Turn it on before installing the next lamp.

When all the lamps are installed, turn on the circuit power at the service panel

and turn on the wall switch. If any of the lamps don't light, check if the switch on the lamp is turned on. Also check that the lamp is properly seated in the track. When everything is working, adjust the lamps to shed light exactly where you want it.

Connect wires from ceiling box to feed connector.

Install cover over feed connector and box.

Insert lamp in track and rotate to lock in place.

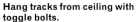

Home office planning

Peripherals

Working from home has become a practical option for many people. And even those who commute to the office usually need some place at home where they can catch up on extra work and sort through personal papers. Homework and hobbies put the younger members of the family in a similar position.

Increasingly, these activities are centered on a computer and a network of other electronic equipment. Whether you make do with a corner of the dining room table or have the luxury of a dedicated workspace, some planning—and maybe new wiring—will avoid a tangle of wires and some severely overloaded receptacles.

Workstation
Specially made units can greatly improve efficiency.

Lighting your office
Use dedicated task-lighting to illuminate the work area without creating distracting reflections. A portable desk lamp is one option, or you could install a small spotlight above the desk. A dimmer switch that controls the room lighting will allow you to set the best level of light for the time of day or the task at hand.

To assess the number and the locations of the receptacles, first plan your office layout to make the best use of the space available. Think about where your desk or worktable should be. You will probably want to take advantage of natural light—but before you make any permanent alterations, try out the position of your computer monitor to avoid reflections from windows and fixed lighting.

A place for your computer

Most people can work comfortably on a desk or table that is 28 to 30 inches high. Ideally a computer keyboard should be slightly lower. This is why manufactured computer workstations are usually made with a slide-out keyboard shelf that can be stowed beneath when not in use. Make sure to get a comfortable chair. And if your children are likely to use the same workspace, chose a chair that is adjustable in height.

A work surface needs to be at least 24 inches deep to provide enough room for the average computer and related add-ons. You'll also need extra space for papers and reference books, plus shelves and drawers to store items like stationery, computer disks, and typical office supplies.

Even the most sophisticated computer is of limited use without some accessory devices. You'll need a printer for any number of tasks and you may want a scanner for putting your own photos and graphics onto the computer. But a printer and scanner only scratch the surface of the world of computer peripherals. CD burners, DVD burners, video game hardware for the kids, external hard drives, and more are all waiting to clog your workspace.

The cable jungle
Each new piece of equipment needs a power supply and a connection to the computer—which is why so many home offices end up with a tangle of wires and overloaded receptacles.

To reduce the number of cables, you could get a new computer with more of this extra stuff already installed. But if you're not in the market for one right now, consider adding some more receptacles to the room. If your home office is directly above a basement, adding the new outlets and the wiring that connects them isn't very hard, expensive, or time consuming. And if your office is on the second floor, under an attic, the job isn't much more difficult. Just run a cable from the service panel directly to the attic. Then fish the cable down to the receptacles.

Also consider installing surge protectors on any receptacle that serves a computer. Fluctuations in voltage are not uncommon, and some of these can damage your equipment.

USB hub
This small hub allows you to connect several pieces of equipment to a single port on the back of your computer.

Installing telephones

Telephone lines used to be just for talking on the phone. But now they're used for transmitting documents, images, e-mail, and accessing all kinds of information from the Internet. In fact, for some people their place of work can be just about anywhere as long as a phone is close at hand. If you want to improve the phone system in your home, now is a great time to do it. All the hardware you need is readily available and none of this work is difficult.

Most homes already have two phone lines, even if only one is in use. So if you just want to add a second line you're set. But if you want two or more additional lines, the phone company will have to run new cable to your house.

Running new line

In most houses, there's a phone-company circuit box installed in the basement. This box carries two lines from the telephone pole. So if you want a second line, you just have to open this box, take out the old cable, and run new cable into it.

To install the cable, first feed it into the end of the circuit box through the rubber gasket that's mounted there. Then strip about 3 inches of sheathing from the cable, and about ¾ inch of insulation from each wire. This wire is very fine, so be careful when you strip it. It's easier to cut the wire off than it is to remove the insulation. Once the stripping is done, loop the wire ends around the matching color terminals in the box and tighten the terminal nuts.

Then run the new phone line to the jack location. Staple the cable every 8 to 12 inches along the floor joists. And drill holes through the joists, as required, to reach the jack location. Once you're there, drill a ³⁄₁₆-inch hole through the floor and into the room. Feed enough cable through this hole to reach the jack. Then staple the cable to the joist as close to the floor hole as possible.

Slide new cable through rubber gasket on end of circuit box.

Strip sheathing from new cable and insulation from wires.

Run new cable to jack location and staple it to joists.

Installing jacks

There are many different kinds of phone jacks available, and even more accessories for the jacks. But for basic two-line service, a duplex jack is a good choice. This unit has two separate receptacles, so you can make individual connections to two separate phone lines.

To install one, mount the jack on the baseboard molding with the screws provided with the jack. Then feed the phone cable into the bottom of the jack and strip the sheathing off the cable. Also strip about ¾ inch of insulation off the wires. Attach the wires to the matching-color terminals and tighten the terminal screws in place.

Use pliers to remove the knockout on the bottom of the jack cover. Then screw the cover onto the jack and test the jack. If a line is not working, check for loose terminal screws.

Mount jack on baseboard

Strip wires and hook on terminals

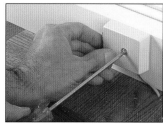
Screw cover onto jack

Outdoor wiring

If you can do your own wiring inside your house, you can certainly do it outside too. The principles are the same. Because outdoor wiring is exposed to all kinds of weather, it must be impervious to water. It must also be resistant to the effects of extreme hot and cold temperatures. Knowing how to work with these materials is most of what you need to know to run electricity outdoors.

Connecting to the house circuits

You can bring indoor electricity outside with one of two exterior fittings:

90° fittings

If you are starting with a new circuit in the breaker panel or tapping into an existing circuit with a junction box, the fitting you will use to get through the house wall will be an LB box. An LB allows you to come through an exterior wall and make a 90-degree turn along the wall. It is

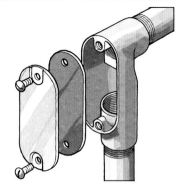

An LB allows you to wire at a 90° angle.

threaded on each end to accept conduit adapters or pipe nipples. Because it creates a 90-degree turn, its front can be removed so that you can help the wires make the turn. The coverplate for this opening fits over a rubber gasket, which makes the box watertight.

An LB is always installed between two pieces of conduit. In some cases, an LB might fit back-to-back with a junction box just inside the wall. Because no splices with plastic connectors are allowed inside smaller LBs, the conversion between cabled wire and individual wire should be made inside the junction box. If you want to exit a basement wall below ground level, do not use an LB. Use instead a junction box mounted to the inside wall, then run conduit through the wall.

Extension boxes

If you are tapping into an outside outlet or light fixture, you will not need an LB. Instead you can sandwich a weatherproof extension box between the receptacle or fixture and its outlet box.

To install an extension box, shut the power off, remove the coverplate and receptacle or fixture, and pull the wires out of the box. Then screw the extension box to the outlet box mounted in the wall. Bring the conduit into the extension box and pull the conduit wires through the opening so that you can work on them comfortably. Join all same-colored wires to pigtails with plastic connectors. Attach the pigtails to the receptacle or fixture.

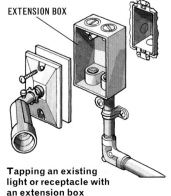

EXTENSION BOX

Tapping an existing light or receptacle with an extension box

Working beyond the house
All outdoor wiring must be encased in conduit unless it is buried 30 inches deep. All fixtures and boxes, including switch and receptacle boxes, must be weathertight and rated for exterior use. And all floodlights and their sockets must be rated for exterior use. As long as you satisfy these requirements, the improvements you make can be as varied as your outdoor needs.

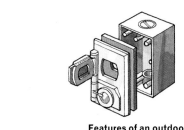

Features of an outdoor receptacle box

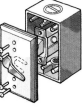

Features of a switch with an external lever

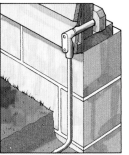

Features of an outdoor floodlight box

An LB and a junction box, back-to-back

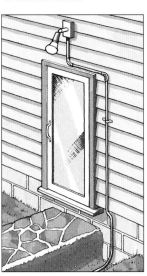

Connecting a new circuit
A box extender and metal conduit

Outdoor receptacles

If installing an outside receptacle mounted to your house would make your outdoor cooking or lawn and garden work easier, you will be happy to know that the job is not that difficult. In most cases, tapping an existing circuit will work. Before you cut into any wall, however, shut the power off.

Installing an outside receptacle

Start by finding a receptacle on the inside near where you would like one on the outside. Then take careful measurements and mark the box location on the outside of your home. Hold a cut-in box against the siding and trace around it to mark the cut. To keep the corners neat, drill each with a ¼-inch bit. Drill completely through the siding and the sheathing. Then use a sabre saw to cut the box opening.

With the opening made, probe through it to find the existing box. If insulation is in the way, push it up and away from your work area. Then go back inside and remove the receptacle from the existing box and open a new knockout hole at the bottom of it. Push a short length of cable through the knockout opening until you think you've pushed enough to reach the new box. Then go back outside and pull the cable out through the opening.

With the cable in place and the new box ready to install, pull the insulation back down. Insert the cable through a knockout opening and mount the box in the wall. Install a GFCI receptacle in the box and add a watertight cover box to keep the rain out.

Installing a GFCI

Every exterior receptacle or fixture must be protected from ground fault. When installing a new circuit, you might install a GFCI breaker, but when wiring only one box, use a GFCI receptacle. A GFCI receptacle senses any imbalance between the positive and neutral sides of the circuit.

When an imbalance occurs, as it does with a short, the sensing mechanism immediately interrupts the flow of electricity.

The only real difference between installing a GFCI and a standard receptacle is that a GFCI often has leads.

GFCI receptacle
This protects the outlet it is in and all outlets after it on a circuit.

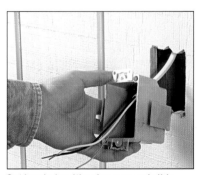

Cut box hole with sabre saw and slide cable into box; push box into hole.

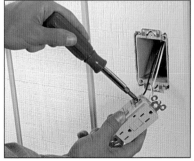

Attach wires to GFCI receptacle, then attach receptacle to box and add watertight coverplate.

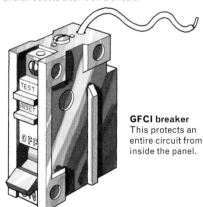

GFCI breaker
This protects an entire circuit from inside the panel.

Outdoor receptacles

Installing isolated receptacles

If you cut your grass with an electric mower, or if you need an electric trimmer to reach under a backyard fence, you should consider installing receptacles nearer your work. All you need is a few weathertight receptacle boxes, conduit, type UF cable, and the willingness to dig a trench between your house and the new receptacle locations.

Once you know where you plan to access the power from inside the house, mark this location on the outside of the foundation wall. Then drive a stake in the ground at this point and another where you want your first outdoor receptacle and stretch a string between the two. If you want more receptacles, run a string between each location.

Begin digging the trench by using a spade to cut the sod about 4 inches deep and 12 inches across. (If you do a neat job of cutting the sod, when you replace it, your lawn will look much better.) Once cut, dig up the sod and pile it on one side of the trench. Continue digging until the trench is about 18 inches deep along its entire length. To protect your lawn, pile the loose dirt on pieces of newspaper or a tarp placed on the opposite side of the trench from where you piled the sod.

With the ditch ready, run plastic conduit between the house and the receptacle locations. Cut the conduit with a hacksaw. At every receptacle location, sweep the conduit up out of the ground with premolded bends called "factory elbows." Then use another bend to re-enter the ditch in the direction of the next receptacle. Factory elbows are connected with glue. You can install the electrical cable in the conduit after all the conduit is in place. But it's easier to slide the cable through the conduit before the fittings and pipe are glued together.

To secure the conduit risers, or bends, slide a concrete block over each set of risers and pour concrete into the block cavities. You don't need to wait for the concrete to set. Go ahead and fill in the trench with the loose soil.

Tamp the soil with your feet until it is firm, then replace the sod and give it a good watering.

With the conduit and supports in place and the wires ready, install a weathertight junction box on each set of two risers. Use plastic fittings that screw into the box and glue to the conduit risers. Of course, at the end of the run, you will have only one riser.

All that remains is to install the receptacles and weathertight coverplates and connect the conduit cable wires to the circuit in the house.

Other outdoor options

Other electrical options might include a string of landscape lights or a front-yard pole light. The installation of these fixtures does not differ substantially from that of the receptacles described here. The same basic techniques are used to carry power to outbuildings or storage sheds. Just remember that all wiring, except low-voltage systems, must be encased in conduit, and all fixtures must be impervious to water.

Inserting the cable
Slide the cable through as you go.

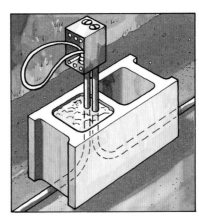

Supporting the conduit
Fill block cavity with concrete.

Working with conduit

Not many residential electrical improvements will require the use of conduit, but some will, and you should know what is available and how to use it. Conduit is required any time individual wires are run in place of cabled wire. It is also required when a cable or wire is in danger of being cut, torn loose, or stepped on, that is, when it is in harm's way. There are several different types of conduit.

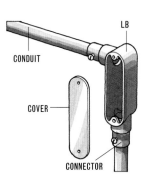

Metal conduit can be bent

Types of conduit

There are three basic types of conduit: galvanized metal, galvanized flexible metal, and plastic. All have at least two variations in wall thickness.

Metal conduit comes in 10-foot lengths and in three wall thicknesses. The heaviest is rigid metal. Rigid is usually hand-threaded and put together with threaded fittings. Because it is so heavy, you have to bury it only 6 inches deep in outdoor installations. The next heaviest metal conduit is known as "intermediate weight." It can be bent with a bending tool, so fewer fittings are needed. It can also be threaded for use with threaded fittings. The lightest weight metal conduit is called "thinwall." It is put together with threadless fittings. It can be bent and shaped to follow the contours of any wall, ceiling, or floor. Both intermediate and thinwall conduit must be buried at least 18 inches deep when used outdoors. Thinwall conduit is also prohibited for underground use in areas that have acidic soil compositions.

Flexible conduit resembles a hose more than a pipe. It is available in two thicknesses. It is very flexible and does a good job in protecting lead wires into appliances such as disposers, water heaters, and dishwashers. The NEC allows the heavier version to be buried, but many local ordinances disallow it for use underground. Flexible conduit is connected to appliances and outlet boxes with special clamp connectors.

As with plumbing pipes, plastic conduit is popular with homeowners. The reason is simple: Plastic conduit does not have to be shaped and can be glued together. (Electricians can shape plastic conduit with special benders that heat the pipe until it is malleable.) When you want a bend in a plastic pipe, just buy a bend fitting and glue it in place. These fittings, called factory elbows, are available in 45-degree and 90-degree angles. Plastic pipe is especially handy when running wire underground and along support beams inside buildings. Because it is not as rigid as metal conduit, it should not be used out in the open where it cannot be secured to walls or other rigid supports. It must be buried 18 inches deep when used underground.

All conduit can be cut with a hacksaw or a sabre saw equipped with a metal cutting blade. After each cut, trim the sharp burrs off the conduit before running any wire through.

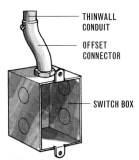

LBs make fishing at right angles easy

Attach conduit to box with connector

Tee fittings join three pieces of conduit

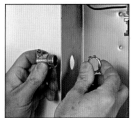

Offsets keep conduit tight against walls

Connector joins conduit to panel

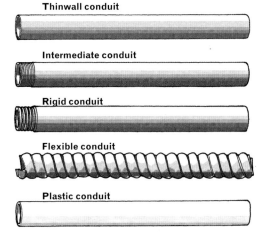

Thinwall conduit

Intermediate conduit

Rigid conduit

Flexible conduit

Plastic conduit

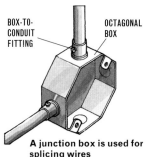

A junction box is used for splicing wires

Installing a floodlight

There's no better way to extend the day than with a house- or garage-mounted floodlight. Aside from offering a measure of security and safety, a floodlight can also improve a wide range of outdoor activities, from backyard barbecues to nighttime dips in the pool, to after-dark driveway basketball games, and even to cooler-temperature, late-night gardening. If none of these ideas appeal to you, rest assured that most of them will appeal to the kids around the house. And to top it all off, floodlights are usually easy to install just about anywhere.

Floodlight options

Floodlights take a variety of forms and are installed in a variety of ways. A quick trip to your local home center will reveal several design options. There are traditional fixtures, like the one shown above, and rectangular quartz fixtures. Some mount on the wall, others in the roof soffit, and still others have motion-activated switches. All do have one thing in common, however: they're designed for outdoor installations and so their components are weathertight.

Access to power

In many cases the easiest access to power is through the garage. Unfinished garages make the wiring a breeze, especially if you don't mind having the switch in the garage. If this doesn't work for you, your next best choice is a ceiling fixture on a circuit that has room for another light.

Once you pick your circuit, shut off the power to it and remove the light fixture. Remove one of the knockouts on the side of the box and install 14/2 with ground cable into the box **(1)**. Attach it with a cable connector. Strip the sheathing off the cable and strip about ⅝ inch of insulation off each wire. Join the black cable wire to the black hot wire in the box with a wire connector. Do the same thing with the neutral cable wire and the neutral box wire. Join the cable ground wire to the other ground wires in the box. Replace the light fixture.

Run the cable to the switch box location and run the same-size cable from the switch location to the floodlight box location. Bore holes through framing members as needed **(2)**, and staple the cable in place at least every 4 feet.

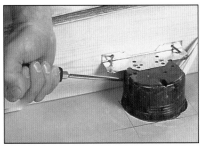

1 Find power source and knock hole in box

2 Run cable through framing members to switch

Installing the fixture

The typical floodlight fixture consists of a metallic weathertight box, two adjustable lamp holders, a rubber weather gasket, and a coverplate. To keep water from entering the box through the cable opening, it's a good idea to install a plastic conduit nipple into the back opening on the box **(3)**.

Drill a hole through the side of the house and pull the switch cable through this hole. Then slide the floodlight box over the cable and push the nipple on the back of the box into the hole. Screw the box to the side of the house.

To wire the fixture, first join the cable ground wire to the grounding lead on the fixture and to a grounding pigtail with a wire connector. Then attach the pigtail to the grounding screw at the back of the box.

Join the white neutral wire from the cable to one of the fixture leads with a wire connector. Then join the black cable wire to the other fixture lead with a wire connector. Attach the fixture securely to the box **(4)** and screw in the bulbs.

Connecting the switch

If you are working in an open garage you can use a standard switch box for this job. Just nail it to a stud about 48 inches from the floor. If the switch location is in a closed wall, cut a box hole where you want it and install a cut-in box **(5)**. A closed location will require fishing cable through the wall. Pick the most efficient route that does the least damage.

Feed the cable from the floodlight and from the power source into the box and strip the sheathing from both cables and about ½ inch of insulation from each wire. Join the ground wires from both cables to a grounding pigtail using a wire connector. Then attach the pigtail to the grounding screw at the back of the box.

Join both white wires in a wire connector. Then hook the black wire from the power source to one switch terminal and the other black wire going to the floodlight to the other switch terminal **(6)**. Screw the switch yoke to the box and install a coverplate. Turn the circuit power on and test the installation.

3 Thread plastic nipple to back of floodlight box

4 Attach fixture securely to the box

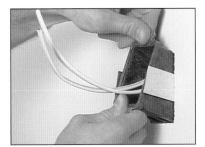

5 Push cut-in switch box into wall opening

6 Attach hot leads to switch

Low-voltage connections

Low-voltage wiring was once limited to doorbells and thermostats. Today, however, low-voltage lighting is being used in places unheard of a generation ago. The reason, of course, is that low-voltage systems give you more light for less money, and rising electric rates have made efficiency an issue. Low-voltage wiring is also safe; if you short circuit a low-voltage system, the shock you get will feel more like a tickle than the life-threatening bite of a 120-volt system. There are literally dozens of low-voltage systems available today, especially lighting systems. Pick whatever you want. None are hard to install.

Deck light

Spot light

Well light

Low-voltage kits

The best way to buy low-voltage components is in kit form. You won't necessarily save money that way, but you won't have to design your own system either. When you buy a kit, for example, the transformer size, the length and size of the wire and the number of allowable fixtures are all figured for you.

Contrary to popular opinion, low-voltage systems can start fires when over-extended. Too many fixtures or too long a run can cause low-voltage wires to overheat. When designing your own system, make sure you use a transformer with a built-in breaker.

If you don't find exactly what you want in one brand, try another brand or another style: track lighting offers a good illustration of this point. Here's just one example. You can get a fixture that fastens to the ceiling and has a surface cord that runs to a receptacle-mounted transformer. Or you can get a system, the same size and similar style that has a surface-mounted transformer that ties directly into the ceiling box, so it's not visible from anywhere.

Mushroom light

Installing a transformer

To reduce house current from 120 volts to 12 volts, a transformer is needed. Most transformers used in home wiring are rated at 100 to 300 watts. The greater the rating, the more 100-foot branch circuits can be served. If a transformer is underrated, the lights it serves will not go on or the wire that serves them will overheat.

Transformers for indoor fixtures can be located in a number of places on or near their fixtures. In some fixtures, they can be part of an electronic circuit (like a stereo's). But in many cases, you will fasten the transformer directly to a 120-volt metal outlet box. Remove a knockout plug and attach the transformer to the box with a clamp. Then join the transformer leads to pigtail connections inside the box. The low-voltage UF wires can then be tied to the transformer's terminals.

A transformer used outdoors, however, must be sealed in its own weathertight box. You can buy transformers with on/off switches built in, or you can use a conventional switch between the outlet and the transformer. The transformer box must be connected to the outlet box with weathertight conduit. Low-voltage UF cable should be laid underground from the transformer to each fixture. Low-voltage fixtures do not need to be grounded, and because they pose no physical threat, do not have to be buried deep or encased in conduit when installed outdoors. But it's a good idea to keep them out of harm's way so you won't to have to repair them after they're installed.

Low-voltage fixture connection

Low-voltage connections are made inside protective boxes on indoor lighting fixtures. In some cases, the low-voltage side of the fixture is wired and sealed at the factory. When you install these fixtures, you only have to wire the 120-volt connection. The terminals on the transformer's low-voltage side can remain exposed as long as the transformer is not covered by drywall or otherwise concealed.

All outdoor connections must be made in weathertight boxes. This can be done the conventional way with binding screws or with special low-voltage connectors that use screw-and-clamp devices. The cable is placed in a slot and the clamp is screwed down over it. As the clamp tightens, it pierces the cable, making contact with the wires inside. In this case, you do not even have to cut the wire at the fixture. Both connections are code approved.

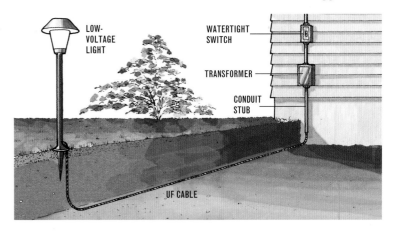

LOW-VOLTAGE LIGHT — WATERTIGHT SWITCH — TRANSFORMER — CONDUIT STUB — UF CABLE

Low-voltage outdoor lights

When it comes to electrical projects, installing low-voltage outdoor lighting is as easy as it gets. These kits are much less expensive to buy and operate than their 120-volt counterparts. A six-head system uses about the same energy as a single 100-watt lightbulb, and the complicated weather protection and shock prevention measures required for outdoor 120-volt systems are almost entirely absent. Low-voltage wires don't even need to be buried deeply; a few inches is all that's necessary.

Installing cable and fixtures

First determine the layout you want and mark the cable route. Do this from the transformer location to the last light. Then use a spade or flat-blade shovel to cut a slice into the ground about 5 inches deep. Push the shovel back and forth to create a V-shaped trench. Lay the cable into the trench, and wherever it sticks up, push it down with a wooden stick. There's really no depth requirement for 12-volt cable. But a couple of inches deep offers the cable some protection and keeps it from being a tripping hazard.

The light fixtures come in different styles. The ones shown here are very common. Each consists of a stake, a riser pipe, and a lamp head. Each lamp head has a lead cable that passes through the riser and is fitted with a cable-piercing connector.

To install the fixture, first drive the stake into the ground a couple of inches away from the cable. Make sure the stake is plumb, otherwise the lights, especially if they're lined up in a row, will look sloppy. Then slide the lamp head onto the riser tube and join the two with the set screw on the riser. Take this assembly and attach it to the stake, again by tightening a set screw.

Drive stake into ground

Connect lamp head to riser

Shopping for fixtures
There are just two basic categories of low-voltage lighting products . At the low end are the familiar packaged kits, consisting of a transformer, cable, and six to eight plastic light heads. The head designs may vary and some kits come with light sensors that can automatically turn on your lights, but the difference is mostly cosmetic. These kits are a snap to install and are very durable.

Your other option is an a la carte mix of cast-aluminum fixtures. These lamps are much more expensive, but they usually look great, the lights are generally brighter, and you often have a bigger selection of styles.

Wiring the transformer

The transformer needs to be installed next to an outdoor receptacle. In most cases, all you have to do is screw the transformer box to the house wall and plug it into the receptacle. But systems do vary, so follow the instructions that come with your unit.

Next, bring the low-voltage cable up to the bottom of the transformer box and cut it to length. Split the last 2 inches of cable in two and strip about ½ inch of insulation off each wire. Crimp a ring connector (usually provided with the kit) onto the end of each wire. Then hook these connectors onto the transformer terminals. Install the transformer cover.

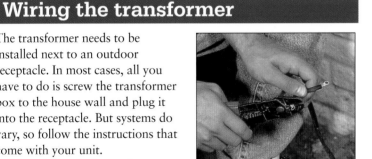

Attach ring connectors to ends of cable wires

Attach cable-wire connectors to transformer

Wiring fixtures

To make the fixture and cable connections, begin by checking that the cable lead from the fixture rests in its slot at the base of the riser. Then expose several inches of buried cable and lay it across the connector fitting on the end of the cable lead. Thread the fitting cap onto the fitting. As the cap is turned down, it pushes the cable into two sharp prongs that pierce the cable and the contact wires.

Make sure lead cable fits in riser slot

Lay cable in connector and tighten cap

Installing a backup generator

There's nothing like a power outage to make us realize how much we rely on electricity. It powers the furnace, the refrigerator, the TV, the computers, the lighting circuits, and in many homes the water well that supplies the showers and toilets. A prolonged power outage can leave us cold, hungry, bored, unwashed, uncomfortable, and largely in the dark.

While an inexpensive portable generator will power the TV and a lamp or two, what's really needed is a unit that's large enough to keep some of the most important circuits running. A good-size generator that can handle these circuits is not cheap, but neither is a long outage in bad weather, when the family has to stay at a motel and eat every meal in a restaurant.

Estimating needs

The output of a generator is rated in watts. This figure indicates the maximum power that the unit can deliver. To determine the wattage of the generator you need, total the wattage of the fixtures and appliances you'd like to power. Then add about 20 percent as a reserve to handle increased startup demand of most electrical motors. Here's an example of how this works: let's say

you wanted to power at least two lighting circuits (240 watts), a sump pump (1500 watts), a refrigerator (600 watts), and a blower on a gas furnace (1200 watts). This gives a total of 3540 watts without reserve power. With about 700 watts of reserve added in, the total comes to about 4250 watts. This is the minimum-size generator this example requires.

Transfer switch

You must connect a generator to your home's wiring system in a way that's safe and efficient. To do this, you need a manual transfer switch that routes electricity from either the power company or the generator to important house circuits.

A manual transfer switch is actually two switches (or breakers) positioned side by side in an auxilary panel. One breaker is powered by the main service panel and the other by the generator. Both breakers can feed power to the circuits, but not at the same time. The key to the system is a rocking toggle clip that connects both breakers in such a way that when one is switched on, the other automatically shuts off.

While both can be off, only one can be turned on at a time. This design protects the generator if it's still connected when the power comes back on. But more importantly, it protects any power workers from exposure to current from the generator when they are working on the system outside the house.

A transfer switch does not automatically route the circuits to the generator when the municipal power fails. You have to manually flip the switch to the generator mode. Then you must plug in the generator and start the engine. When municipal power returns, you have to stop the generator and flip the switch.

Wiring the switch panel

Mount the transfer switch panel next to the main service panel. Then shut off the power at the main panel and remove a knockout plug from the facing sides of both boxes. Mount a short threaded nipple between the two. Run a piece of 10/4 cable through the nipple and strip the sheathing from both ends. Connect the neutral and ground wires to the main panel's neutral bus bar. Then attach the red and black wires to a 30-amp, 240-volt breaker. Snap this breaker onto the hot bus in the main panel. Connect the cable to the transfer switch box in the same way.

Identify the circuits you want to move and remove the wires from the main panel breakers and the neutral bus bar. To bring the discontinued circuits into the switch panel, they must be extended. Many local codes allow you to join these cable wires to extension wires, using wire connectors in the main panel. Others require that you pull the disconnected cables from the main panel and put them in junction boxes to make the connections to extension wires. Once the extensions are attached, install these circuit wires in the switch panel.

1 Attach pipe nipple to hole in side of main panel.

3 Pull 10/4 cable from one box to the other through nipple.

2 Slide switch panel over other end of nipple; screw to wall.

4 Attach circuit wire to new breakers in switch panel.

Connecting the generator

The way a portable generator is hooked to the transfer switch box is best determined by consulting with local code officials. Some areas allow hookups to a proper size receptacle (mounted in a watertight box) by means of a heavy-duty extension cord made of 10/4 cable. Other areas require a generator cord be hard-wired directly into the house electrical system. Check with the appropriate city and state agencies before you make the connection.

If local codes permit, make extension cord for generator hookup.

Overhead garage doors can be dangerous things. Just ask emergency room attendants about crushed fingers. These injuries occur when people try closing sectional garage doors by sticking their fingers into the gap between panels and pulling down. Naturally, the gap closes. Electric garage-door openers solved this problem, but created another: serious injuries to children who have been trapped under doors when the openers bring them down.

Because of these injuries, door-opener manufacturers have made real strides in safety.

Auto-reversing mechanisms are now standard. As soon as the door hits anything above floor level it automatically reverses. And openers now come with infrared sensor units that are installed just above the floor. When the infrared beam between the units is interrupted by an object or a person, the door stops automatically and then reverses.

Controls

When shopping for a garage-door opener, you'll find many control options. In addition to operating the power unit and the light fixture (both manually and remotely), some systems allow you to hard-wire a passage door so the light comes on for 5 minutes after the passage door is opened. The options you choose will dictate how the unit is wired. Follow the manufacturer's instructions carefully.

Even though specifics change, the general approach is fairly consistent. Current to the power unit comes via a power cord that's plugged into a ceiling-mounted receptacle. The infrared sensors are mounted just above the floor, where the door comes down, and are joined to the power unit with a low-voltage cable. The power unit is controlled by remote units and by a fixed, keypad control unit that's usually mounted on a wall in the garage.

Preliminary considerations
With redundant safety mechanisms built in, there is little chance that a door opener will cause serious injury or damage. That's the good news. The bad news is that equipment that's designed to be sensitive requires careful adjustment and a good door that works properly. If your garage door could use some adjustment, consider calling a professional door-repair technician before installing a new opener. Door adjustments are not as easy as they look and they can be dangerous if not done properly.

Hanging the opener

The first step in the installation process is to assemble the opener components according to the manufacturer's instructions. Then you must establish the center of the door opening and hang the support bracket on the door header at this center point. Once the bracket is in place, lift the idler-arm assembly into the bracket and secure it with a locking pin.

Lift up the power unit and idler-arm assembly and rest it on top of a step-ladder. Then fabricate a support bracket for the power unit using perforated angle iron. There are a number of reasonable support hanger designs. One good one is to attach a 3-foot-long 2 x 4 block to the ceiling using 4-inch-long wood

screws driven into the joists above. Then attach two angle-iron support legs to the block using ¼-inch lagbolts.

Lift the power unit up and attach it to these hangers using the hardware supplied with the opener. To keep the power unit from twisting during operation, install a diagonal brace made of angle-iron between the two support legs.

Attach the door to the traveler arm that's connected to the opener. Then check that all the bolts joining the door panels are tight. Do the same with all the hardware that's supporting the door tracks. Once the power is hooked up, test the door operation to make sure it's working properly.

Attach infrared sensors to brackets mounted on wall studs next to garage door.

Attach the low-voltage cables from both infrared sensors to the back of the power unit.

Make any necessary performance adjustments by turning screws at the back of the power unit.

Slide the traveler assembly onto the end of the track tube about 40 inches from the power unit.

Carefully slide the capped end of the track tube into the bracket on top of the power unit.

Bring the chain around the drive sprocket on the power unit, making sure all links are engaged.

Lightning protection

Lightning should be considered a very real electrical threat to every home. It can melt circuit cables, destroy the electrical components in appliances, injure or kill inhabitants, and, of course, burn a house to the ground. A well-grounded home has better protection against lightning than a poorly grounded one. Houses with lightning rods connected to heavy grounding conductors are even better protected. And those with lightning arresters installed in their service panels or at their meters are safest.

Grounding antennas

TV antennas and satellite dishes can attract lightning, which can blow the circuitry of a television connected to an ungrounded dish or antenna. If you have either, make sure it is grounded properly.

To ground an antenna just fasten an approved clamp to the frame of the antenna, near the bottom. Then run a No. 6 ground wire to a second clamp fastened to a copper-clad grounding rod just below grade.

Because some satellite dishes do not have grounding terminals, you may have to improvise a connection. The best method is to drill and tap a ¼-inch hole in the support post and fasten the ground wire to the frame with a brass bolt. Then run the No. 6 bare wire to an approved clamp

and ground rod. Again, the rod connection should be made just below grade.

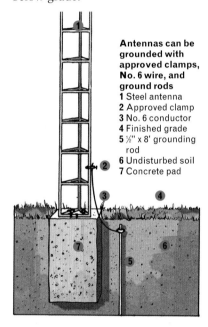

Antennas can be grounded with approved clamps, No. 6 wire, and ground rods
1 Steel antenna
2 Approved clamp
3 No. 6 conductor
4 Finished grade
5 ½" x 8' grounding rod
6 Undisturbed soil
7 Concrete pad

Grounding aluminum siding

Because metal sidings can attract and conduct electrical charges generated by lightning, the NEC suggests that all metal sidings be grounded. If your siding is not grounded, tuck a No. 10 bare wire under the lip of the bottom-most layer of siding and secure it about every 10 feet with sheetmetal screws. From the No. 10 wire, on two opposing corners of your home, run a No. 6 wire down to a copper-clad grounding rod. Use approved clamps and

bury the connection just below grade.

When installing new siding, run a grounding wire around the perimeter of your home under the first layer of siding. For added protection, run wires vertically from the perimeter wire to the soffit at 10-foot intervals. Secure these wires by wrapping them around the siding fasteners as you go. Finally, attach the perimeter wire to grounding rods on two opposing corners of your house.

Lightning arresters

A lightning arrester is a small rectifier that routes a high-voltage lightning charge away from an electrical system and into the earth. Lightning arresters are inexpensive and are not that difficult to install. Because they must be installed on the hot side of a home's main disconnect switch, however, you will have to have the power to your home shut off by your local utility or a licensed electrician. Never attempt to install a lightning arrester with the power on.

With the power off, locate a knockout plug on the top of your service panel the size of the threaded nipple on your arrester. Remove this plug and insert the nipple through the opening. Then tighten the arrester in place with the provided fastening nut.

Next, slide the white wire from the arrester under an unused terminal on the neutral bus bar and tighten the terminal screw. Then loosen one of the terminal screws on the incoming side of the main disconnect switch. Slide one of the black wires from the arrester under that terminal, next to the incoming service wire already in place, and retighten the screw. Finally, fasten the other black arrester wire under the remaining disconnect terminal.

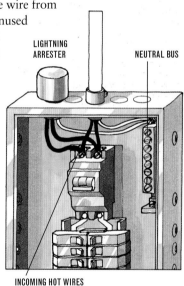

LIGHTNING ARRESTER

NEUTRAL BUS

INCOMING HOT WIRES

Before calling for an inspection, use a torque wrench to make sure that the two main disconnect screws are very tight. Because manufacturer specifications vary, check with a local electrical supplier to find the proper torque rating for your panel.

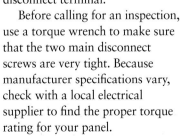

Electrician's tools

ELECTRICIAN'S TOOLS

You need only a fairly limited range of tools to make electrical connections, but an extensive general-purpose tool kit is required for making cable runs and for installing electrical accessories and appliances.

SCREWDRIVERS

Buy good screwdrivers in a range of sizes for tightening electrical terminals. Fixed-blade screwdrivers and multibit versions with interchangeable tips stored in the handle are both handy to have.

Insulated and noninsulated screwdrivers

An electric circuit should be turned off before working on it. But it's still a good idea to use a fully insulated screwdriver. An insulated screwdriver has a plastic handle and a plastic insulating sleeve on its shaft.

Use an ordinary noninsulated screwdriver with a bare shaft for general work such as fastening mounting boxes to walls.

KNEEPADS

Protect your knees when working on outlet receptacles and other devices or appliances near the floor.

Flashlight

Keep a flashlight handy for checking your service panel when a fuse blows or breaker trips. You may also need extra light when working on connections in the basement or attic (a flashlight that stands on its own is particularly helpful).

WIRE CUTTERS

Use wire cutters for cropping cable and flex to length.

- **Essential tools**
  Screwdrivers
  Wire cutters
  Wire strippers
  Power drill and bits
  Flashlight
  Voltage tester
  Continuity tester
  General-purpose tools

Electrician's side-cutting pliers

These are heavy-duty pliers that have large jaws and shears and padded handles. You can use them to cut wire and cable.

Diagonal cutters

Diagonal cutters will cut thick conductors more effectively than will electrician's pliers, but you'll need a hacksaw to cut heavy cable, flexible conduit, and other metal components.

WIRE STRIPPERS

There are various tools for cutting or stripping the plastic insulation that covers cables and flexible cords.

Multi-tool

Wire strippers

To remove the insulation from cable, use a pair of wire strippers with jaws shaped to cut through the covering without damaging the conductor. There is a multipurpose version that can cut screws and conductors and strip insulation.

Utility knife

A knife with sharp disposable blades is best for slitting and peeling the sheathing around electrical cable.

DRILLS

When you run circuit wiring, you need a drill with several special-purpose bits for boring through wood and masonry.

Auger

Some electricians employ a long wood-boring auger to drill through the wall plate and framing when they're running a switch cable from an attic down to its mounting box.

Power drill

A cordless power drill is ideal for boring cable holes through framing and for securing junction, receptacle, and switch boxes in place. As well as twist bits and screwdriving bits, you'll need auger bits and perhaps carbide-tipped bits for boring through brick walls.

If you shorten the shaft of a wide-tipped spade bit, you can use it in a power drill between floor joists.

TESTERS

Even when you have turned off the power at the service panel, use a tester to check that the circuit is safe to work on.

Voltage tester

Be sure to buy a twin-probe tester that's intended for use on a household electrical system.

Always check that the tester is functioning properly before and after you use it by testing it on a circuit you know to be live.

Following the manufacturer's instructions, place one probe on the neutral terminal and the other one on the live terminal that is to be tested. If the bulb illuminates, the circuit is live; if it doesn't illuminate, try again between the ground terminal and each of the live and neutral terminals. If the bulb still doesn't light up, you can assume the circuit is not live, provided you have checked the tester.

Continuity tester

A continuity tester will indicate whether current will pass from one terminal to another, so it's ideal for diagnosing short circuits, broken wires, or improper grounding. Alternatively, buy a multitester that combines the functions of continuity testing and voltage testing.

Using a continuity tester

The following is an example of how a continuity tester can be used. Be sure to switch off the power at the service panel before making any tests.

To determine whether two accessible cable ends are part of the same cable, twist two of the conductors together at one end. Then apply the tester's probes to the same conductors at the other end (1) and depress the circuit-testing button on the tester. The bulb should light up and, with some testers, there may also be an audible signal. Untwist the conductors. Then make the test again. If the bulb doesn't illuminate, the two ends belong to the same cable.

To check whether a plug-in appliance is safely grounded, apply one probe to the ground pin of the plug and touch an unpainted part of the metal casing of the appliance with the other probe (2). Depress the test button. If the ground connection is good, the bulb will illuminate.

Don't use the appliance if the bulb illuminates when you apply the probe to either of the plug's other pins (3). If the appliance is defective, have it repaired by a service technician or simply replace it with a new one.

1 Apply a probe to each conductor

2 Test ground pin and casing

3 Test one other pin and casing

GENERAL-PURPOSE TOOLS

Every electrician needs tools for dealing with the house structure as it affects running cable and securing electrical components.

Claw hammer

For nailing cable straps to walls and framing.

Hand sledge

A heavy hand sledge is used for driving cold chisels and for a variety of demolition jobs.

Cold chisel

Cold chisels are made from solid-steel-hexagonal-section rod. They are used, among other things, for cutting through old electrical components, plaster, and brickwork.

Slip a plastic safety sleeve over the chisel to protect your hand from a misplaced blow with a hammer.

Wood chisels

For notching and trimming house framing.

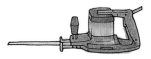

Power jigsaw or reciprocating saw

For cutting through walls and floors and making other miscellaneous cuts.

Floorboard saw

This is the best tool for cutting across a pried-up board.

VIAL

Level

For checking that mounting boxes are secured plumb.

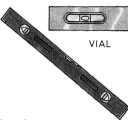

Drywall knife

For making wall repairs after installing boxes and cable.

Adjustable wrench

A single adjustable wrench is easy to carry and handles the wide range of hexhead fasteners that might be encountered.

Glossary

B

Blocking
A short piece of wood between studs or joists, providing extra strength to a framework.

BTU
British Thermal Units. The amount of energy required to raise the temperature of one pound of water by 1 degree Fahrenheit. Used as an energy-rating guide to air conditioners and other appliances.

Burr
The rough, raised edge left on a workpiece after cutting or filing.

C

Circuit
A path through which electricity flows.

Conductor
A component, usually a length of wire, along which an electrical current will pass.

Cornice
The decorative molding course between walls and ceiling.

Cove molding
A decorative molding with a concave section or with a trough for hidden lighting.

E

Extension
A length of electrical cable for temporarily connecting an appliance to a wall socket. Also, a structural addition to an existing building.

F

Flashing
A weatherproof junction between a roof and a wall or chimney, or between one roof and another.

Fuse box
The service box where the main electrical service is connected to the house ciruitry.

G

Galvanized
Covered with a protective coating of zinc.

GFCI
Ground fault circuit interrupter.

Ground
A connection, as a wire, or rod, that provides a path of least resistance connecting electricity with the earth, providing a safety feature.

I

Insulation
Materials used to reduce the transmission of heat or sound. Also, nonconductive material surrounding electrical wires or connections to prevent the passage of electricity.

J

Jamb
A vertical upright that forms the side of an opening, or the framework of the opening as a whole.

Joist
A horizontal wooden beam used to support a floor or ceiling.

L

Lath
Narrow strips of material nailed to walls, joists, etc., to provide support for plaster.

LB box
An electrical housing which allows you to connect electrical conduit at right angles.

N

NEC
National Electrical Code.

Neutral
The part of an electrical circuit that carries the flow of current back to source. Also, a terminal to which the neutral connection is made. Alternatively, a muted color.

P

Positive
The part of an electrical circuit which carries the flow of current, also called live.

R

Raceway
A channel for holding electrical cable.

Rafter
One of a set of parallel sloping beams that form the main structural element of a roof.

Retrofit
To refit a mechanism or structure so that it will have added qualities or capabilities.

S

Sheathing
The outer layer of insulation surrounding electrical cable. Also, the outer covering of a stud-framed wall that is applied beneath the wall siding.

Short circuit
The accidental rerouting of electricity to ground which increases the flow of current and blows a fuse.

Soffits
The underside of a part of a building such as the eaves, or archway.

Sole plate
The sill of a stud partition, also called bottom plate.

Studs
The vertical members of a stud-framed wall.

T

Terminal
A connection for an electrical conductor.

Thermostat
A temperature-regulating mechanism.

V

Valance
A decorative banding for curtains and window openings.

VOM
Volt-ohmmeter, a device which measures electrical resistance in ohms.

W

Wall plate
A horizontal member placed along the top of a wall to support the ends of joists and spread their load.